The POWER Series

SAS

Great Britain's Elite Special Air Service

Leroy Thompson

Motorbooks International
Publishers & Wholesalers

First published in 1994 by Motorbooks
International Publishers & Wholesalers, PO Box 2,
729 Prospect Avenue, Osceola, WI 54020 USA

Motorbooks International books are also available
at discounts in bulk quantity for industrial or
sales-promotional use. For details write to Special
Sales Manager at the Publisher's address

Library of Congress Cataloging-in-Publication Data
Available

ISBN 0-87938-940-0

On the front cover: Members of the SAS Pagoda
Troop prepare to go through the windows, which
have just been blown, of the Iranian embassy in
London. *Special Air Service*

On the frontispiece: Member of the Special Air
Service SP Team demonstrates the equipment worn
for counterterrorist operations. Note the Range
Rover used to transport the teams in the
background. *Special Air Service*

On the title page: Training in the tire house. The
technique of clearing rooms in pairs developed by
the SAS is now used by most hostage rescue units.

On the back cover: SAS Counterrevolutionary
Warfare assault gear, circa 1980, includes antiflash
hood, gas mask, ballistic vest, H&K MP5, Browning
Hi-Power, and spare MP5 mag pouch. Note the
spare Hi-Power magazine on the wrist for fast
access. *Ken MacSwan illustration*

Printed and bound in Hong Kong

Contents

WHO DARES WINS

Preface

When David Stirling formed the Special Air Service (SAS) in the Western Desert during World War II, he knew he was creating a unique military unit—unique in both mission and composition. Initially formed to threaten Gen. Erwin Rommel's extended Afrikakorps supply lines, the SAS would assume all sorts of behind-the-lines missions, including airfield raids, which ultimately destroyed more than two entire Luftwaffe Geschwader of approximately 100 planes each. As the SAS mission evolved during the war, it included other types of raids as well as intelligence missions. On the continent of Europe, SAS members worked with the resistance against the Germans as well as carrying out raids preceding D-Day. As the Allies rolled toward victory, SAS Jeep Patrols ranged ahead of the advancing armies gathering intelligence and hunting down Nazi war criminals. Stirling's concept had evolved as the war progressed, but what had allowed this evolution was the selection of rugged individualists who could still function as members of a team, men with the versatility to evolve along with the missions assigned them.

Stirling had also foreseen a meritocracy where ability took precedence over rank or title. In the British Army—where officers had enlisted personnel assigned as servants and class divided ranks just as class divided British society—this was quite a revolutionary concept. Nevertheless, this radical concept worked—and has continued to work throughout the history of the SAS. As a result of this system, highly motivated and intelligent NCOs have been attracted to the SAS with the realization that their abilities will be recognized and appreciated. On the other hand, officers lacking the ability and self-confidence to lead by example or to bow to superior knowledge and experience on the part of their NCOs have normally stayed with more traditional regiments.

Through the half century since the formation of the SAS, the Regiment's mission has expanded to include counterterrorism, counterinsurgency, deep penetration raids and intelligence gathering, bodyguarding heads of state, acting as trainers for foreign special forces, designating targets for smart weapons, and providing the "teeth" for British intelligence operations. Even as the mission has expanded, however, selection standards have remained high. Service in the SAS has almost become a prerequisite for certain careers after military retirement in Great Britain, too. Executive protection, counterinsurgency training, and high-level security consulting are the purview of former SAS members, and normally once someone has served in the SAS, he will maintain close ties with the Regiment. As a result, the distinction between official and unofficial operations sometimes becomes hazy. Loyalty among members of the SAS is high—so high that after World War

SAS's famed winged dagger insignia, although initially the "dagger" was intended to represent Excalibur.

SAS member having a "cuppa" illustrates the sand-colored beret, blue stable belt, and SAS parachute wings. Ken MacSwan illustration

II, a special unit of the SAS continued until the 1950s to hunt and, in some cases, execute Nazis who had implemented Hitler's "Commando Order" against special forces personnel.

Secrecy has surrounded the SAS to such an extent that until the rescue of hostages at Prince's Gate in London, few outside the mili-

tary special operations community even knew of its existence. So shrouded in mystery was the SAS that when the first Americans carried out exchange training, upon their return, many assumed their SAS service had been with the better-known Scandinavian Air Services. Secrecy has also added to the SAS's mystique, particularly in Northern Ireland, where the Irish Republican Army (IRA) considers the SAS its principal Bogeyman and has tended to blame much on it.

As with many special operations units, the secrecy surrounding the SAS has created myths about the men who wear the sand-colored berets. In some cases, truth is more incredible than myth, but the SAS style is certainly not one to court publicity. On the contrary, members of the SAS are conditioned to avoid the limelight. Pride in the Regiment is such that headlines such as, "Yesterday, a team of what were reportedly SAS members carried out a successful raid behind enemy lines" are about as much publicity as most SAS members will ever get, certainly until their careers are over. Within the small special forces community, their accomplishments are known and appreciated and that is considered far more important than plaudits of those who don't really understand the pride and professionalism which motivates them to undergo the selection and training necessary to serve in the SAS.

Perhaps the best way to summarize the respect with which the SAS is viewed by special forces of other nations is the fact that imitation truly is the sincerest form of flattery. Australia and New Zealand have their own SAS units; Rhodesia formerly had the SAS and the Selous Scouts; South Africa has Recce Commando units based on the Rhodesian SAS and Selous Scouts; the United States' Delta Force bases itself in many ways on the SAS; France, Belgium, and Greece have special forces based on their World War II SAS units; and numerous other countries have used the SAS as the pattern for their special forces.

In writing this work, the author has attempted to shed light on various aspects of SAS training, tactics, and operations without compromising the Regiment's ability to carry out future missions. Information is in some cases drawn from open sources and in others from less-available sources. Much material comes from conversations on long plane rides to far-off places with strange-sounding names or over meals between the author and friends in the SAS. Having served on numerous training teams over a twenty-year period with active and retired members of the SAS, the author has had a unique chance to understand the evolution of SAS tactics and doctrine. Photographs of SAS personnel are always sensitive due to the fact that members of the Regiment will often serve on undercover operations. As a result, in a few situations, faces may be blacked out or photos in which the faces are not visible will be chosen. For the same reason, photos illustrating certain tactics or training methods may be chosen from those in which former SAS members are instructing foreign military personnel or police in their methods.

The SAS motto, "Who Dares Wins," has become both a source of pride and, at times, grim humor among members of the SAS. In tough situations, it has been known to be corrupted to "Who Cares Who Wins?" Other versions of the motto containing great truth are "Who Thinks Wins" or "Who Sweats Wins," as hard work, both mental and physical, are key elements in SAS training. The fact that civic action "hearts and minds" campaigns often are important components of SAS counterinsurgency warfare operations might lead to the conclusion that "Who Wins Cares." A sense of carefully calculated daring has certainly always been important in SAS tactics, because it minimizes the risks before action. Hopefully, this book will give some insight into why the SAS is, indeed, daring and special.

The author as a member of a mixed training team, including former SAS members, demonstrates SAS building clearing techniques to members of a US Army Hostage Rescue Unit. The tire house is another type of training facility allowing the capability to shoot in all directions.

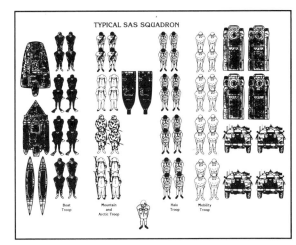

Typical SAS Squadron organization. Ken MacSwan illustration

Chapter 1

Selection and Continuation Training

The SAS selection course does not rely on a battery of psychological tests or high-tech computer profiles but on a procedure that has been used with slight modification for decades. The rugged Brecon Beacons and Black Mountains of Wales are the site of this selection procedure and, oddly enough, were originally chosen because they tested skills deemed necessary for SAS operations in the jungles of Asia. Although at first obscure, there is an odd logic here, as jungle, desert, or the Brecon Beacons requires a combination of outstanding land navigation skill and stamina to traverse.

In virtually every conflict in which they've been engaged, the SAS has had to fight and survive in a hostile environment; hence, the Brecon Beacons test the mental and physical stamina of candidates as well as their land navigation skills. Even without formal psychological profiling, experience has yielded a psychological profile of those who successfully complete the selection process. They will normally be intelligent, assertive, self-sufficient, emotionally stable, forthright, and alert. They will neither be excessively introverted nor extroverted and will not be dependent on orders to know what to do. They will also retain their sense of humor under adversity.

Candidates for the regular SAS—22nd SAS Regiment—may apply from any regiment of the British Army, including the Territorial Army (TA) Regiments (equivalent to US Reserves), Royal Air Force, or Royal Navy. For the two TA SAS Regiments—21st and 23rd—candidates may apply directly from civilian life. To apply for one of the two four-week-long selection courses run in winter and summer of each year, officers must be between the ages of 22 and 34; those applying from other ranks must be between 19 and 34. Either must have at least three years left to serve. A good record with a previous regiment is assumed. Although candidates have traditionally come from all regiments, in the last decade there has been a large influx of former Parachute Regiment soldiers, pushing that composition of enlisted personnel to just over fifty percent. Before being accepted for a selection course, candidates first receive a briefing at Stirling Lines, the home of 22nd SAS, on the regiment's mission and what will be expected of them during selection. They then must undergo a physical examination and a standard Army physical fitness test.

Officers do their Test Week in the third week and enlisted personnel do theirs in the fourth week, as officer candidates must undergo an additional test known as Officers' Week. Experienced noncommissioned officers (NCOs) from the SAS Training Wing run the selection courses. During the leadup to Test Week, candidates are up at 0400 and on the go until at least 2200 every day. Throughout the process, their abilities to learn quickly and self-reliance are observed and tested. The leadup period stresses

SAS personnel learn all sorts of insertion techniques, including fast roping from helicopters.

map reading and navigation using watches and compasses. Members of noninfantry regiments normally have to work harder to gain such skills rapidly. During this period, the candidates are well fed, with diets rich in high-protein foods to give them extra stamina for what they will face. Training is progressive: distances, loads carried, need for individual initiative, and time constraints get tougher as the weeks progress. During exercises, candidates have to move from rendezvous point (RV) to rendezvous point, receiving their next RV from a training NCO at each point. Hill runs and river crossings will be included. By the end of the second week, those candidates remaining will be doing 15-hour marches per day. At about this point SAS humor usually holds that SAS stands for "Savage and Sadistic."

In the third week for officers and the fourth week for other ranks, candidates face the famous "Long Drag," the final grinding march during which they have to cover 60km, carrying 25kg rucksacks as well as 5kg more on their belts plus their rifles, in fewer than 20 hours. Weather in the Brecon Beacons can be harsh, and candidates have died on the selection course. Additionally, rain makes clothing and rucksacks heavier and footing uncertain. Since part of this final march includes Pen-y-Fan, the highest peak in the Brecon Beacons and noted for its sheer sides, footing becomes an especially important consideration. No matter what the weather, however, the selection course goes on. The SAS attitude is that war isn't postponed for rain or snow, and neither is the selection course.

During the last two decades, certain changes have been made in the final slog of Test Week, specifically in the use of "sickeners" to try to force candidates to drop out. The most infa-

Members of the SAS work constantly on land navigation, though they are taught not to mark on a map or fold it in such a way that their objective can be determined. Note the use of the grass stem for exact pointing. This technique is also used so no telltale finger grease will indicate an objective on a map in case of capture. Special Air Service

Members of the SAS must not only be able to swim but to swim with equipment.

mous one called for candidates to finish a grueling march, then to see the trucks scheduled to take them back to camp pull away, abandoning them to a long hike back. The idea, of course, was to see who would give up and who would tighten their holds on their rifles, adjust the straps on their Bergen rucksacks, and resume walking. By the way, "tighten their holds on their rifles" is correct, as the SAS normally doesn't use slings, believing correctly that a slung rifle isn't much good in combat. Therefore, while trying to crawl up sheer inclines during selection, candidates must carry their rifles in their hands.

Beginning in the 1970s, however, sickeners were dropped and the training NCOs began using positive motivation to encourage candidates to succeed. Many old-line NCOs felt this was really just a concession to a softer breed of young soldiers, but others thought it kept many promising recruits from being eliminated. An-

SAS instructors are in demand throughout the British and US Armed Forces. In this case, a former senior noncommissioned officer in the Special Air Ser- *vice, left, instructs US Army personnel in close-quarters battle.*

other change was in the weight placed in the rucksacks. Previously, numbered bricks drawn from quartermaster stores were used to make up a candidate's load. Now, however, useful items such as clothing and food fill the rucksacks. Those who have previously done the course often give those preparing for the final test hints on what to include. High-energy candy bars are popular, and many have included olive oil on the theory that soaking the socks with it cuts friction.

Land navigation remains important, and candidates undergoing the Long Drag have to check in at RVs along the route. At this RV, tasks to test their abilities to function when tired and under stress have replaced the old

sickeners. Candidates might be asked to assemble foreign weapons or answer questions about world affairs.

Candidates for the Territorial Army (TA) SAS Regiments complete their selection over ten successive weekends. If at any point in the procedure they are deemed unsatisfactory, they're asked not to return for the next weekend. The final Long Drag for the TA has traditionally been slightly easier, with the rucksack lighter and the distance less—although it is still a formidable selection course.

Other ranks successfully completing this final slog are now ready for the next phase of their training, but officers must still face what is known as Officers' Week, which tests their ability to lead experienced and highly skilled SAS NCOs and troopers. During this week, officers who have already successfully completed the Long Drag must demonstrate their leadership, tactical planning ability, and briefing skills. They must plan an SAS-style raid and brief experienced NCOs on it, then take their questions. These questions will be tough, based on the NCOs' experience of such operations, and test an officer's poise and self-confidence as well as planning ability. So tough is the process that only about six percent of officers attempting selection for the SAS successfully complete it. In fact, there is often a shortage of SAS junior officers due to the tough selection procedure and the fact that junior officers are required to rotate out of the SAS after one tour, although they may return later to command a squadron. Selection remains tough enough that there has recently been a shortage of other ranks successfully completing selection, especially with the retirement in the mid-1980s of many long-serving SAS soldiers.

Other offshoots of the SAS use similar selection courses. The Rhodesian SAS, for example, used to incorporate land navigation and their own version of the Long Drag, but also included a raid on a high-security installation, planned and led by the officer candidates and carried out by enlisted candidates. The Australian SAS runs basic selection courses similar in nature, but screens candidates first with interviews and psychological tests. Australian officer selection is especially rigorous, as they first have to go through a tough Officers Selection Course. Those successfully completing this course are then eligible when a slot opens in the Regiment, whereupon they undergo basic selection with the other ranks. Not only does this system ensure good officers, but the fact that the officers normally can take the lead in the basic selection course, having already completed an even-tougher one, gains the respect of those they will command.

Other countries' special forces have adapted the SAS selection procedure to fit their own environments. The famed Rhodesian Selous Scouts, for example, incorporated land naviga-

Members of the Selous Scouts field dress a monkey. The SAS and its offshoots put great stress on being able to live off the available flora and fauna of any area of operations. David Scott-Donelin

tion and long marches, but also included the necessity to live off of the land and survive on small amounts of food during the selection process. The addition of hunger as a dimension

Rapid and accurate use of the H&K MP5 is one of the premier SAS close-combat techniques.

not only served to show that a Scout could survive on far fewer calories than normally ingested, but also brought home the point that when hungry, food avoided before can become delicacies. Throughout Selous Scouts selection, for example, a dead monkey hung in the center of the camp, rotting as each day progressed. As the candidates grew more ravenous, the monkey grew riper. Finally, their first real meal in days was provided by cooking the maggot-infested monkey. In addition to learning that one will eat almost anything when necessary, they learned that even tainted meat can be eaten if thoroughly boiled, although it should not be re-heated a second time. They also learned that maggots can be a good source of protein. South Africa's Recce Commandos, heavily influenced by the Rhodesian SAS and Selous Scouts, also use an SAS-style selection course.

The MP5SD, the suppressed version of the MP5 used for special operations.

Among other units trained along SAS lines that also use similar selection procedures are the Malaysian Special Service Group, the Pakistani Special Service Group, the Omani Sultan's Special Force, the US Delta Force, and the New Zealand SAS. The New Zealand SAS Group includes a pre-selection course by the end of which candidates are expected to be able to cover 32km cross country with an 18kg pack in fewer than six hours. The nine-day selection course includes exercises to test intelligence, stamina, and will to prevail. To simulate the need to transport supplies in rough terrain, for example, candidates may have to carry fuel cans full of sand across 16km of sand dunes. This and other slogs will likely come after only two or three hours sleep. Officers have added the necessity to evaluate intelligence information, plan operations, and give briefings, as in

22nd SAS, to experienced NZ SAS NCOs. The final Long Drag covers 56km. The final stage of the selection course also includes escape and evasion. Normally, fewer than ten percent of NZ SAS candidates are selected. Those who are candidates for the TA SAS have to undergo exactly the same pre-selection and selection courses as members of the regular NZ SAS.

Once they have successfully completed the selection course, candidates for the SAS move on to continuation training, where they will learn the basic skills of the special forces soldier and continue to be evaluated. So important does the SAS consider training that as they leave the Training Wing, members of the Regiment see a sign reading, "Death is nature's way of telling you that you've failed selection." Continuation training itself lasts fourteen weeks, followed by six weeks of jungle training and, for those not

The SAS's special counterterrorist training target used here incorporates both a hostage and a hostage taker so that head shots are required.

17

The SAS Operations Research Unit has been impressed with the Steyr AUG, and it is now used for certain missions by the SAS.

already parachute-qualified, four weeks of parachute training. Only after successful completion of these twenty-four weeks does the soldier become fully "badged" as a member of the SAS, entitled to wear the sand-colored beret and winged dagger badge.

SAS training is a tried and successful combination of theory, practical demonstrations, and hands-on practice. One of the first and most critical skills learned is that of operating in the standard SAS four-man patrol. Patrolling and reconnaissance are critical parts of this phase. Trainees first learn how to determine where to establish camouflage observation posts to gather intelligence without being detected, especially by thermal imagers. They then practice setting up such posts and undergo lengthy training inside, as constricted conditions may become a way of life if these posts have to be maintained for weeks at a time. In the Falklands, Northern Ireland, and Iraq, for example, soldiers had to eat, sleep, and perform bodily functions in these cramped "hides."

Trainees learn three main types of observation posts, though variations may be construct-

ed to fit specific terrain situations. Most compact of the posts is the "Top to Tail," in which four men lie head to feet, facing in alternate directions. Those on each end will normally handle observations in each direction, while the two in the middle either rest, record information, or communicate with their base. In the second, "Pairs" layout, two men face each direction in an elongated hide, often with their equipment at their feet. One man facing each direction observes, while the other two rest or process information. Finally, there is the "Star" layout, in which four men face in each of the compass directions. Once again, all four will not be observing simultaneously unless there is a lot of activity going on.

Weapons expertise starts with individual weapons such as the Browning or SIG pistol, H&K MP5 submachine gun, L1A1 SLR (self-loading rifle), Steyr AUG, or M-16 rifle (known in the SAS as the Armalite). Note that the SAS has avoided being saddled with the SA-80 "Bullpup" rifle that proved so disappointing when issued to the rest of the British Army.

Pistols are used as primary weapons on clandestine operations and as secondary weapons in other situations. Rapid target acquisition and engagement, instinctive firing, double taps, rapid magazine changes, malfunction clearance drills, and other basic combat handgunning skills are taught with the pistol. Firing from behind cover, prone, and kneeling, trainees learn to shoot effectively while maximizing their chances of surviving an encounter.

Many of these same basic skills are taught for the submachine gun, although trigger control and the use of laser sights or underbarrel lights are also stressed. The SAS has taught both center-of-the-chest instinctive firing, in which the butt of the submachine gun nestles in the center of the firer's chest, and hip-firing, in addition to standard shoulder-firing techniques, with the submachine gun. Some of these CQB skills, which are particularly applicable to counterterrorist operations, are introduced in continuation training but not really polished until a squadron is on counterterrorist assignment. The

The Steyr AUG is highly thought of by members of the SAS Operations Research Unit

rifle remains the basic weapon and the most stress is placed upon its use during continuation training. Firing from cover and on the move, at ranges out to 500m or more, builds confidence and skill with the rifle. Immediate action drills against pop-up targets, often carried out in patrol formation, build reactions and teamwork. Although the L1A1 is semi-automatic only, the M-16 may be fired on fully or semi-automatic. Therefore, during training, SAS soldiers learn controlled use of fully automatic fire, particularly in counterambush situations or when breaking off an attack. The M-16 with the M-203 grenade launcher is appreciated both for its indirect firing capability with HE grenades and its ability to fire either gas or canister rounds. The SAS has often used shotguns for jungle operations, but M-203s with canisters are becoming more popular. Still, Remington 870, Moss-berg 500, and SPAS twelve-gauge shotguns are still in the armory, and familiarization training with them is part of continuation training. In addition to usage, of course, basic maintenance is taught on all weapons the trainees will use. A familiarity course with foreign weapons, particularly those of the former Soviet bloc, normally rounds out the individual arms portion of continuation training.

Support weapons are of special importance in the SAS, as they act as force multipliers, allowing a four-man patrol to strike with the firepower of much larger units. With their indirect firing capability and portability, mortars are especially invaluable in raiding operations. If necessary, one man can carry the lightweight (6.275kg) 51mm. Trainees learn how to use it with illumination, smoke, and anti-personnel rounds. Much more effective is the 81mm L16.

19

The author undergoing H&K MP5 re-qualification.

Broken into its three main components—the barrel at 12.7kg, the mounting at 12.3kg, and the baseplate at 11.6kg—this mortar can be carried by three SAS soldiers. Among skills taught with the Sight Unit C2 are direct and indirect firing, day or night. In addition to firing skills, drills in rapid assembly and disassembly and long slogs carrying the mortar components and bombs prepare SAS troops to use the mortar in raiding missions of the type they carried out so successfully against aircraft on Pebble Island during the Falklands War. Although the 51mm mortar is much easier to carry, it has a limited range of 750m, while the 81mm can reach 5600m. Among special mortar munitions SAS soldiers learn to use is the Merlin "smart"

radar-guided anti-armor round.

The general-purpose machine gun also offers sustained firepower for ambushes and raids. The FN L7A2 is the primary machine gun for the British Army these days, including the SAS. Rapid barrel changes combined with tactical training in covering fire during withdrawals or sustained fire in breaking an enemy attack prepare the trainees for scenarios in which they will use the general-purpose machine gun. Since portability is as important as firepower, virtually all training with the general-purpose machine gun is done with the bipod rather than the tripod. As with the mortar, drills in carrying the L7A2 long distances, then quickly bringing it into action are of extreme importance. The same

C2 sight used on the 81mm mortar can be used on the general-purpose machine gun to give it indirect firing capability. In the case of both mortar and general-purpose machine gun, drills become patrol activities, as everyone has to help carry mortar bombs or machine gun belts.

Other weapons include the 66mm M72 LAW and its replacement, the 94mm LAW80, both of which, although intended for use against armored vehicles, have always been widely used by Special Forces Troops for "bunker busting" or against any other hardened target. SAS trainees also learn to use the MILAN anti-tank weapon and the Stinger and Javelin air defense missiles. These weapons are relatively heavy for many SAS missions, but if carried in SAS Land Rovers, they could be used in operations behind enemy lines to delay an advance.

Since so many SAS operations take place at night, the use of special night optics or other image enhancement devices both for target acquisition and surveillance make up an important part of continuation training as well. SAS trainees also learn to use the Thorn EMI hand-held thermal imager, the Maxilux M (military) and P (photographic) night vision system, the Spylux personal night viewer, and the Type SS32 or SS69 "Twiggy" (used for calling in artillery, naval gunfire, etc.), all of which are surveillance/intelligence-gathering tools. For sighting weapons, SAS troops receive instruction in such devices as the Orion 80 passive night sight, the H&K aiming point projector, the Kite individual weapon sight, the SS84 lightweight individual weapon sight, and the NVS-700 night vision system. The specific systems are often upgraded as the SAS Operations Research Unit searches for the lightest and best in current technology. The SAS also spends substantial time learning to use laser designation systems for guiding in "smart weapons," a tactic they used effectively against SCUD missile sites and other targets during the 1990-1991 war against Iraq.

The basics of silent killing are also taught during continuation training. SAS Training Wing cadre draw from various martial arts, including jujitsu, karate, and escrimi, as well as

The SAS has used the M-16 rifle quite extensively, including versions with the M-203 grenade launcher.

traditional British close-combat techniques dating back to W. E. Fairbairn and the commandos of World War II. The primary consideration is that techniques be simple and effective. Silent killing techniques are combined with stalking skills, as the approach prior to the attack is critical to making a silent kill. In addition to unarmed killing techniques, the trainees learn how to kill with a blade (the standard thrust to the carotid artery still being one of the best), a garrote (often a survival saw serving a duel purpose), a crossbow or composite bow, an axe, a machete, or a shovel. Practicality and surviving the encounter are the keys of SAS hand-to-hand training. The SAS close-combat philosophy is

21

Training in using cover while firing the M-16 (usually known as the Armalite among SAS).

thirty different types of radios makes instruction even more difficult. Burst transmission systems such as the MEROD have become more important in SAS clandestine operations and, as a result, more time is spent in learning their use. The trainees are also taught special SAS radio codes and techniques of calling in air or artillery strikes. Throughout this phase of training, instructors remain alert for those candidates showing special proficiency so that they can later be trained as signalers.

All trainees learn the fundamentals of field medicine, so that they will know how to deal with an emergency when far away from medical help. Those who are selected as medics will receive more intensive training later. Basic sanitation and preventative medicine when operating in the jungle or other hostile environments are also covered. Included in preventatives are knowing such simple field-expedient ways of killing intestinal worms as ingesting a couple of tablespoons of kerosene or gasoline, as well as being aware of the danger of insect bites and the necessity for taking chloroquine to prevent malaria. Normally, the individual medical kits will contain dressings and bandages, morphine syringes, some type of antiseptic (potassium permanganate has often been used by the SAS since it can also be used to start fires, for signaling, and to purify water as well), an antidiuretic, an antiseptic burn cream, an antibiotic, and an oral pain killer such as codeine. The ability to make improvised splints or stretchers from available materials is considered an extremely important SAS skill and is covered in basic medics and expanded upon during later training exercises. One of the most common problems the SAS will have to deal with is traumatic wounds; hence, medical training stresses that a soldier must first restore and maintain breathing and heartbeat, stop bleeding, protect wounds or burns, immobilize fractures, and treat shock. Throughout, improvisation is emphasized. For example, in sterilizing and cleaning burns, if water is scarce, urine may be used, as it is quite sterile, and because maggots eat dead tissue only, they may also be used to fight infection.

simply that there are no dangerous weapons, only dangerous people.

All SAS members also learn communication skills with a variety of radio equipment, so that they have the skills of normal Army radio specialists, and those who become signalers will gain even more expertise. Even though the rest of the British Army no longer uses Morse transmission, SAS personnel must be able to transmit Morse code at the rate of eight words per minute. They are also taught how to use sophisticated satellite systems and methods for constructing aerials in jungle, desert, or mountains to extend a radio's range. The fact the SAS uses

Basic demolitions training teaches the primary types of explosives and how to place them for best effect. Slab forms of C3/C4 and TNT are the two most widely used explosives by the SAS, but trainees also learn how to use electrical and nonelectrical detonators to initiate the explosives. The many uses for detonating cord are one of the most important aspects of this section of training, as this versatile detonating device can also be used in booby traps, secondary killing grounds in ambushes, and various other deadly ways. In addition to learning the methods of placing explosives, SAS trainees also learn how to choose the most effective targets for sabotage, ones that will have a domino effect on the enemy's war effort. Blowing up a locomotive, for example, stops one train, while blowing up a critical railway bridge stops all trains. Attacks on airfields remain a favorite mission of the SAS, harking back to their beginnings in World War II, so placement of charges to crater runways, collapse hangers, and ravage aircraft is covered in some detail. As with other aspects of SAS training, patrol exercises will often be tailored around a scenario involving infiltration to a site, then sabotaging it. In simple terms, at the end of continuation training, an SAS soldier should be able to choose a target, select the correct type of explosive, compute the correct amount of the explosive needed, position it for the most effect, and detonate it. Creation and avoidance of booby traps is also covered in this section. Mines will be important in operations behind enemy lines, so the trainees learn types and placement of antivehicular and antipersonnel mines, as well as various types of improvised explosive devices. Grenades and pyrotechnics are also part of their training.

Throughout instruction, aptitude and skill evaluation tests are given along with initiative exercises designed to force the trainees to put into practice skills they have learned. In the past, these included escaping from high-security prisons or infiltrating defense installations, but are now under direct control of the Training Wing and often will require a patrol to work as a team. For example, patrol members might have to transport a mortar and mortar bombs across a chasm using rope bridges or across a river or stream. Such tests allow the Training Wing cadre to evaluate the trainees, while continuing to teach them.

One of the most interesting and most important aspects of SAS continuation training is survival training, during which the soldiers learn to live off the land in all types of environment. Although the edibility of insects, birds, and animals not normally found on most menus is the most notorious part of this sections, the ability to fish or trap small game as well as recognize edible flora makes up a much larger portion of the course. Basically, the survival course teaches SAS soldiers how to find food, fire, shelter, and water. The section dealing with food teaches the acquisition of meat by tracking animals, constructing snares and traps, hunting, as well as field dressing and preserving meat, and fishing with nets or traps or by other methods. Edible plants in different climates make up the rest of the section on acquiring food. More esoteric foods such as insects and reptiles are covered, with hints on which to eat and which to avoid and how to prepare them (when consuming worms, for example, first let them starve to clear their insides, then dry and grind them into a powder for use in soups and stews). In addition to choosing a safe place to build a fire, the basics of fire making include gathering tinder, kindling, and fuel sources (animal droppings as well as wood, coal, oils, and animal fats). Various methods to spark a fire, from windproof matches to a fire bow and drill or a lens, are taught. The type of shelter depends on the area of operations, but certain basic premises concerning where to camp apply everywhere. SAS soldiers will become familiar with root and bough shelters, natural hollows combined with fallen trees, saplings combined with parachutes or ponchos, lean-tos, and other types. For tropical operations, bamboo shelters are explained, while for Arctic operations, snow caves, and igloos are illustrated. Obtaining water and retaining fluids are among the most important of all survival skills and are stressed accordingly. Collecting rain, using solar stills, gathering water from plants, melting ice and snow, and more extreme measures such as sucking moisture from animal eyes and bodies, all offer possibilities for obtaining this absolute necessity. Loss of body fluids will also create a need for salt, a lesson driven into SAS trainees, who learn how to locate natural salt licks, to obtain it from sea water, to recognize salt-containing plants, and to use animal blood as a source of salt. As will be discussed in the next chapter, once assigned to a troop, SAS soldiers will learn additional survival skills tailored to their troop's mission.

The final section of continuation training is Escape and Evasion (E&E) and Resistance to Interrogation (RTI). During this phase, trainees learn techniques of escaping captivity and avoiding recapture, including methods for dealing with guard dogs. An old SAS story and an incident that happened to the author illustrate the effectiveness of this training: Some years ago, members of 21 SAS were training in Denmark, acting as infiltrators while the Danish Home Guard practiced hunting them down. The Danes refused to carry out similar exercises in the future, however, because too many of their aggressive attack dogs had been killed by the Sassmen. Likewise, the author, who was trained in this technique for dealing with dogs, was attacked by a German Shepherd, part of a pack of semi-wild dogs, one night and rendered it *hors de combat* very quickly.

During the E&E exercise, trainees are given outdated military clothing and dropped off in a remote area. Whether they are given a knife and compass or not is somewhat at the whim of the training cadre. An infantry battalion acts as a security force attempting to capture them. Those who are captured must undergo interrogation, but so do those who escape capture. The interrogation usually lasts only about 24 hours but seems endless. Various techniques are used, including sensory deprivation, hooding, and forced standing or squatting. Candidates will be interrogated by experienced interrogators from Military Intelligence or MI5; facing female interrogators after being stripped nude adds a level of humiliation. Throughout this phase, candidates are not allowed to reveal any information

except traditional name, rank, and serial number. If they do reveal anything else, they are immediately RTUed (Returned to Unit), meaning they are out of the SAS and sent back to their previous regiment. Although not as harsh as the treatment an SAS soldier might expect to face after being captured, this training does remove some of the fear of the unexpected that accompanies capture and interrogation. It also gives members of the SAS an incentive to avoid capture. Reportedly, the training has worked quite well in the cases of SAS captured in the Falklands and Iraq. Although treated harshly, none broke.

E&E and RTI survived, candidates move on to Brunei, where they will undergo jungle warfare training. Brunei holds special significance as a jungle warfare training center since it is also the site of the SAS's most recent jungle campaign against the Indonesians between 1963 and 1966. Special emphasis is given to land navigation in the jungle and to ambush and counterambush skills. The jungle training section ends with a final four-man patrol exercise.

Those who are not already parachute-qualified move on to RAF Brize Norton, home of the British basic parachute school, to undergo jump training. During this four-week course, eight jumps will be made, the first from a tethered balloon, a long-standing British airborne tradition. The remaining seven jumps will be from a C-130 and will include one night jump and one "operational" jump meant to simulate a real parachute insertion.

These various hurdles passed, the SAS soldier is now "badged" and joins his Sabre Squadron, where he will continue to hone his troop and individual specialty skills, as well as cross training, for another two to three years before he can really be considered a fully trained operational SAS operative.

Rappelling has proven to be an important skill for members of the SAS, whether for counterterrorist operations or climbing in the Falklands or Oman. US Army

Chapter 2

Cross Training and Troop Training

Training will continue throughout a soldier's career with the SAS. Once assigned to a troop, that training will focus on two primary areas: his specialty within his patrol and his troop's specialty. Within the SAS, organization is based on multiples of four. The patrol consists of four men: a medic, a linguist, a demolitions specialist, and a signals specialist. After a soldier has been with the Regiment for awhile, he will normally be trained in more than one specialty so that there is redundancy in skills within each patrol in case of casualties. Four patrols make up a troop, and four troops make up an SAS Sabre Squadron. In each troop there will be one officer, who functions as a member of one of the patrols in addition to commanding the troop. Each of the four troops also has a specialty: HALO (parachute), Boat, Mobility, or Mountain. Normally, those soldiers who have been with the SAS for some years will have served in more than one troop as well and, thus, can combine skills when special operations are called for. Those who have served in HALO and Mobility Troops, for example, would be well trained to carry out a freefall insertion into a desert environment, then survive and fight there for extended periods. Likewise, those who have served with Boat and Mountain Troops would be particularly well qualified for insertion by small boat into an Arctic environment. Four

Members of HALO Troops give the SAS the capability of inserting personnel with less likelihood of detection.

Sabre Squadrons—A, B, D, and G—combine to make up the 22nd SAS Regiment, and there are other specialized subunits, such as Operational Research, Counterrevolutionary Warfare, and Intelligence (known as the "Kremlin" in the SAS), as well as a special signals unit—264 (SAS) Signals. The missing C Squad-ron, by the way, was the basis for the Rhodesian SAS.

Although there are many similarities between the SAS and the US Army Special Forces, one notable difference is in the specialist skills. Within the Special Forces A Detachment, for example, there will be a team commander, a second in command, an intelligence specialist, two communications specialists, two medical specialists, two engineering/demolitions specialists, two weapons specialists, and an operations specialist. To some extent, the larger size and more diverse skills of the Special Forces A Detachment are predicated on the team's primary mission of raising and training guerrilla units. Special Forces Operational Detachment Delta, which is formed much along SAS lines, has an organization more similar to that of the SAS. Within the SAS patrol, it is assumed that everyone is proficient enough with weapons to teach this skill if necessary, and it is assumed that all will function skillfully at gathering intelligence. Due to his close contact with the local population, in fact, the patrol medic will often become the *de facto* intelligence specialist.

Training and cross training in the specialties build on the basic skills in those areas learned during continuation training. Medics,

Members of an SAS HALO Troop illustrate full HALO kit from the front, rear, and side. Note the oxygen mask, altimeter, goggles, and reserve chute in the front view and the SLR and pack in the rear and side

views. During HALO jumps, shifting of such equipment as the rifle and pack can cause death or injury.
Special Air Service

for example, work in hospitals and, in some cases, participate in the US Army Special Forces' year-long "bush doctor" training course. They are also in charge of the much more comprehensive medical kit for the patrol, which is designed to allow the medics to perform surgical or dental procedures when operating away from medical assistance. Medic training stresses the use of medical assistance as part of a "hearts and minds" counterinsurgency campaign. Particularly in medical civic action programs, SAS "bush doctors" have to know how to dispense medicine and deliver babies. More than one SAS medic now has children in Borneo or Dhofar named after him as a result of this latter skill.

Demolitions specialists learn specialized techniques for blowing up bridges, docks, and all sorts of other structures, as well as how to use cutting or entry charges to blow in doors or walls. For those times when the patrol is operating behind enemy lines away from resupply, the demolitions specialists will also learn to make various types of improvised detonators and explosives. SAS demolitions specialists become artists with detonating cord, which they can link to multiple charges. Sophisticated explosive charges, such as cone-shaped ones that deliver a very exact cutting explosion with minimal residual destruction, are within the repertoire of the demolitions specialist. Redundancy is also taught to make sure that once emplaced, explosives go off. Therefore, at least two separate detonation systems will be used. Specialized techniques particularly suited to the patrol's likely mission will be learned and rehearsed. For example, remembering the SAS's classic role as aircraft raiders, demolitions specialists learn to destroy aircraft by affixing small charges in the cockpit, on the undercarriage, and to the nosecone. Fuel dumps and tanker trucks on airfields are also prime targets. SAS demolitions specialists also learn their limitations; for example, that they probably won't be able to carry enough explosives to blow up a tunnel, but that a train destroyed inside a tunnel can effectively block it until cleared. Bridges may be blown by charges at

Members of SAS HALO Troops are familiar with all types of parachutes, including the easily steerable Ram Air-type such as this.

behind enemy lines, they can control entire radio nets which they may well have established after having trained the operators. They will know more cryptography than other members of the patrols and will be able to encrypt and decipher communications as necessary. The A-16 HF transceiver used by the SAS between the 1960s and the 1980s aided encryption with a built-in dial for encoding Morse, but as radio interception techniques have grown more sophisticated, so has the training for SAS signalers. Among the techniques they learn to protect their communications are frequency hopping, digital encryption, and various other anti-jamming and low probability of intercept techniques, as well as such mundane tasks as the proper leveling technique when setting up a portable satellite communications terminal. It will normally fall to the patrol signaler, too, to call in aerial resupply, medical evacuation, or patrol evacuation.

SAS linguists normally learn languages whenever possible from natives of the areas being studied. The Royal Army Education Corps' School of Languages instills the initial training, but SAS soldiers are then expected to work on fluency. After experiences in Malaya where the ability to speak the local language not only paid dividends in winning "hearts and minds" but also in gathering intelligence, stress on language skills became even greater in the SAS. When time allows, each member of a Sabre Squadron is given language training prior to deployment, and when this is not possible, the linguist on the patrol teaches his comrades. In some cases, they work in small groups with tutors but will also attend language schools such as the US one in Monterey, California. Language specialties within the SAS tend to reflect the areas in which the Regiment has traditionally operated; thus, Arabic and Malay are well-represented. And since it was often assumed that the SAS would be committed on the Northern Front during a Warsaw Pact invasion of NATO territory, it is normally possible to find a wide diversity of European tongues—particularly Russian, German, Czech, and Polish, as well as Scandinavian languages. During the Falk-

each end of a span to knock it down or by blowing the supports at one end and then letting it collapse of its own weight.

Signals specialists fine-tune their already sophisticated radio skills. Not only do they know how to use the various types of SAS radios, but also how to maintain them and how to maximize their effectiveness. When operating

lands War, however, the Regiment did find itself somewhat short of Spanish speakers, but that language has since been added to the list of those regularly studied.

Learning to function as part of a patrol while gaining individual skills is inherent to becoming fully integrated into the SAS. Members of a patrol learn to move in whatever formation best fits the terrain and the likelihood of contact. The file (roughly rectangular), the single file, or the diamond arrangement may be chosen, but in most cases patrol members will space themselves so that a mine, grenade, or mortar round will not injure the entire patrol. To provide all-around defense, the patrol will normally move with a point man, two flank security men, and a "tailgunner." When the patrol must stop, four men maneuver to cover each of the points of the compass for 360 degree security. Avoiding silhouetting themselves against the skyline, staying off trails that may have been booby trapped, and other basics of combat movement quickly become second nature to members of an SAS patrol. The four-man patrol offers a good compromise of mobility, stealth, and firepower. David Stirling originally conceived of a five-man patrol, but four has proven more workable, at least partially because two pairs can "buddy up." Movement at night and silently using hand signals will be practiced until patrol members instinctively know what each will do. Immediate action drills in case of ambush are another important part of patrol training, once again so that each member of a patrol knows what his comrades will do. Normally while moving, each member of the patrol will be aware of certain RVs along the route where they will rejoin should an ambush scatter them. After former members of the Rhodesian SAS and Selous Scouts joined 22nd SAS, Drake shooting drills were added to the counterambush repertoire as well. In this technique, if ambushed, patrol members immediately shoot a couple of rounds into every likely hiding place within their arc of fire as they break away from the ambush. Since the small size of the SAS patrol makes it imperative to break off as soon as possible, however, the Drake technique would

Good view of the altimeter and chronograph formerly used on SAS HALO Troop chutes. MOD

only be used normally on larger "fighting patrols" or when taking fire from all sides. These larger patrols, which may set ambushes, carry out prisoner snatches, or attempt to actively seek out the enemy, will normally consist of two or more patrols or even an entire troop.

31

One of the most important patrol skills remains the establishment of observation posts prior to establishment of which the patrol leader has checked four criteria: Is the objective clearly visible from the observation post? Can clear communications be established from the observation post with the patrol's controlling headquarters or with a relay station? Is the observation post secure from detection by the enemy? Can the patrol live in the observation post for up to a month?

Learning specialized troop skills begins during each soldier's twelve-month probationary period with the Regiment and continues

Members of SAS Boat Troops may be inserted via wet jumps directly into the ocean.

throughout his assignment to a troop. In numbering the troops assigned to a squadron, Freefall is normally first. In D Squadron, for example, no. 16 Troop is Freefall, no. 17 is Boat, no. 18 is Mobility, and no. 19 is Mountain. Therefore, troop skills will be considered in this same order.

The members of HALO Troop learn the advanced parachute skills that enable them to be inserted silently from heights where aircraft noise is not normally audible on the ground, to drop below or off of radar screens, and to be inserted by jumping from across a border, then floating into the target country. The basis for

Just as navigation is an important SAS skill on land, it is also an important skill for members of Boat Troop.

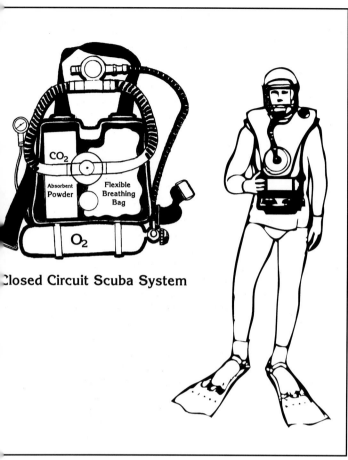

Closed Circuit Scuba System

CO₂

Absorbent Powder

Flexible Breathing Bag

O₂

Layout of the SAS's closed-circuit scuba system. Ken MacSwan illustration

these specialized skills is the six-week HALO course, during which soldiers learn the starfish position used to stabilize a jumper while free falling, as well as how to use the oxygen container for high-altitude jumps, control the 100lb Bergen rucksack during jumps, and prevent such problems as mask icing and frostbite. HALO jumpers must also learn to recognize the various types of hypoxia that can affect them at high altitudes. The first HALO descent is from 12,000ft, and the final one is from 25,000ft. While in freefall, a jumper will be traveling at about 125mph until deploying his chute at

about 2,000ft by an auto release mechanism such as the Irvin Hite-finder D/1 Mk 4. For special mission jumps where the jumpers want to quickly "fall off" of a radar scope, the chutes may be manually deployed at a lower altitude. SAS troops, for example, have practiced jumps into fjords in Norway where the chutes would be deployed very late to prevent radar detection. Normally, the SAS philosophy is that it is virtually impossible to make a parachutist invisible to radar, but he can be made so difficult to detect that most operators will miss him. Jumpsuits made of radar-absorbent material help make the jumpers harder to spot, in effect turning them into "Stealth" parachutists. HALO Troop members often watch jumps on radar screens, in fact, to evaluate the difficulty faced by radar operators in detecting them. During training, HALO Troop puts great stress on night jumps since operationally, it is highly likely that insertions will take advantage of darkness. The ability to land closely together and remain a cohesive fighting unit, always important, must be practiced along with all of the other sophisticated parachuting skills.

In addition to HALO techniques, Troop members also learn high-altitude, high-opening (HAHO) and low-altitude, low-opening (LALO) jumps. In HAHO jumps, the chute is popped after a fairly short freefall—on a jump at 10,000m, for example, the chute would likely be popped at about 8,500m—so that parachutists can have a long glide, perhaps lasting an hour or longer, into an area. For clandestine insertions, especially across a border, this is a very useful technique. HAHO jumpers can travel fifteen to twenty miles from their jump point. LALO jumps allow the plane to fly below a radar screen to insert the parachutists. Using this method, the chute may actually be deployed during the jump to pull the jumper from the plane. The recently introduced Aerazur/GQ Low-Level Parachute was designed especially for LALO operations and can be used as low as 250ft.

Ram air parachutes are normally used for specialized HALO and HAHO jumps, including the GQ Advanced Tactical Parachute System for jumps up to 7700m. Very stable in cross winds and using slotted flaps for braking, this chute allows very accurate, controlled landings. Also used is the Irvin Integrated Free Fall Parachute Assembly Type PB11, Mk1. During the descent while gliding under the canopy, the parachutist travels forward at a rate of about 50mph, while descending at a rate of about 15ft per second. Special systems are also used to deliver HALO Troop equipment, including the BASE (British Airborne Systems and Equipment Ltd.) CADS (Controlled Aerial Delivery System), which consists of a ram air parachute, an airborne guidance unit, and a transmitter. In automatic mode, a remote operator can guide the CADS to within 100m of the landing site, or for even more precise landing, an operator can guide it manually.

Members of the four HALO Troops are responsible for keeping members of other troops within their squadron apprised of the latest developments in airborne tactics and equipment, particularly those who have previously served in HALO Troops and may be called upon to make freefall insertions. A substantial number of the members of the Operations Research Unit will have served in HALO Troops in the past, too, and can apply their experience to evaluating new equipment of possible value.

The SAS Boat Troops are trained to carry out amphibious and SCUBA operations. The idea for forming these troops came about from the traditions of the Special Boat Section in World War II and as a result of the successful operations carried out by SAS patrols with the Royal Marine Commandos in Borneo. A high degree of cooperation remains between members of the Boat Troops and the Royal Marines Special Boat Squadron as well as with the 539nd Assault Squadron, which pilots Rigid Raider assault craft. An entire Boat Troop can be carried in three Rigid Raiders for amphibious infiltration.

Other boats used by the SAS for special operations include the two-man Klepper Canoe, the three-man Mk 13 collapsible Klepper, the three-man Gemini inflatable, and such new high-tech designs as the Subskimmer, which can carry four men on the surface or just below it during infiltrations. The Rigid Raider, howev-er, has proven especially useful due to its speed of 35kn, very silent engine, low profile, and survivability. The latter characteristic was well proven during the SAS diversionary raid on Port Stanley Harbor when Rigid Raiders took heavy fire. Geminis were also used in the Falklands Campaign for landings on South Georgia. SAS Boat Troop members also train on Landing Craft Vehicle/Personnel Carriers (LCVPs), which often transport Geminis to their dropoff point. The heavily armed and armored LCVPs can also wait offshore to give close fire support if needed.

Boat Troop members are trained for SCUBA operations, as well, including closed-circuit SCUBA which has the advantage of not creating bubbles due to the CO_2 produced in breathing being absorbed by a powder inside the apparatus. The lack of bubbles, of course, makes it easier to infiltrate a site under water. Other advantages of the closed-circuit apparatus are that with only a 10–15cu-ft capacity oxygen bottle, the rig is very compact, yet the swimmer can stay under for 3–3 1/2 hours. Disadvantages are that the closed-circuit rig requires a complicated setup which if not performed correctly can result in the death of the swimmer and that if used below 50ft for very long, the pure oxygen being breathed can kill the swimmer as well.

Boat Troop members must also learn specialized skills, such as how to use limpet mines or how to make "wet jumps" directly into the water. In such jumps, the wet suit-clad paratroopers drop their equipment in floatable containers and release their own chutes just before hitting the water. In addition to getting near their target via boat or parachute, they also learn to "lock-in" and "lock-out" of submarines, allowing them to infiltrate using closed-circuit SCUBA after leaving a submerged submarine.

More than any other group, the Mobility Troop reflects the origins of the SAS in the western desert. The "mobility" part of the troop's mission comes from the special vehicles designed for the unit, but the troop could just as easily be called "Desert Troop," as this is the environment they are trained primarily to fight in. Once again, those who have previously served

Members of the Special Boat Squadron, equipped similarly to SAS Boat Troops, come ashore from their Klepper. Note the suppressed Sterling SMG. SBS

in other troops lend versatility, whether to perform a HALO jump into the middle of the desert or to carry out operations in areas such as Oman's Jebal Ahkdar or Iraq, where mountains and desert combine.

Mobility Troop members have excellent desert survival skills, chief among them the ability to conserve and locate water. Water discipline while still maintaining personal hygiene is one of the tricks of operating in the desert, and Mobility Troop medics must make sure that all members of their patrol take care of them-

36

selves, as sores and insect bites in the heat and abrasive sand can soon incapacitate a soldier. Snakes and insects, particularly, can prove the bane of those operating in the desert (but they are also potential sources of culinary pleasure). Clothing must be carefully selected, to keep the wearer cool during the heat of the day but warm during the cold desert nights. Troop members often adopt traditional desert garb such as the Shemagh, and desert boots remain standard footwear.

The principal vehicles used by Mobility Troop are special Land Rovers and the Light Strike Vehicles seen so often in film clips of Operation Desert Storm. Since maintenance depots are often hundreds of miles away, these soldiers must have exceptional mechanical skills as well as improvisational ability to keep their vehicles running. They carry spare parts with them and have become skillful at making rapid repairs while on operations. Their vehicles often incorporate special features to prevent breakdown, too, including oil coolers, oversized radiators, and special tires.

The original SAS desert vehicle during World War II was the Jeep, but the most famous Mobility Troop vehicle was the "Pink Panther" Land Rover used until 1976 for operations in Arabia. Taking its name from the pinkish desert camouflage, this vehicle proved highly effective and was viewed with affection by all members of the SAS. Among its many special features were:

- Front- and rear-mounted general-purpose machine guns, the rear mount designed for 360deg traverse and also able to take a .50 Browning if so desired. The mounts are designed to keep the vehicle stable during firing, as well.
- Front- and rear-mounted smoke grenade dischargers
- 40gal fuel tank
- Special "sand channels" (ramps for getting out of loose sand) on the sides
- Additional 10gal fuel tanks
- Fuel expansion tank
- Hood-mounted camouflage net for covering the vehicle at the approach of aircraft

- Raised vehicle commander's seat for ease of visibility and operation of the front-mounted general-purpose machine gun
- VHF and UHF radios
- Blackout lights
- Spotlight
- Cole sun compass
- Sestrek magnetic compass mounted for easy visibility in front of the driver
- Side-mounted rifle scabbards designed to allow quick access if necessary to bail out of vehicle under fire
- An intervehicle starter socket since dead batteries are a problem in the desert
- Special easy-access storage racks for grenades; spare ammunition; water; fuel; tent; such tools as a pickax, shovel, theodolite and tripod, and tire tools; binoculars; fire extinguishers; and rucksacks. Normal belt order is worn in case it is necessary to rapidly "bail out" under fire.

More recent versions ordered in 1985 have been built on the long Land Rover 110 chassis by Glover Webb. Although the latest version maintains many of the traditional "Pink Panther" features, it also incorporates an electric winch and a satellite navigation system that can pinpoint the vehicle's location within 15m by comparing the signals of four or more satellites. With a full tank, a Mobility Troop Land Rover has a range of about 650km. In addition to knowing how to maintain, load, drive, and navigate their vehicles, members of Mobility Troop must also know how to rig them for parachute drops as well.

Weapons maintenance also requires special care in the desert. Since sand and oil can combine to render a weapon inoperable, oil must be wiped off. One inventive SAS patrol discovered that soaking parts in gin and then air-drying left just a minute amount of juniper berry oil on the moving parts! (Normally, water discipline in the desert preaches the avoidance of alcohol, but these troops may not have wasted the excess gin.) Sand must also be kept out of the bores of the weapons; either special rubber muzzle caps or condoms can be used for this purpose, then shot through if necessary. High tem-

Members of an SAS Boat Troop assemble their Klepper Commando canoe, a job that normally takes 10–15 min. The current version of this canoe incorporates "stealth" design and construction to avoid radar detection. Special Air Service

perature can also increase pressure in ammunition, so it must be stored carefully.

Because they are easily spotted by air while in the desert, Mobility Troop members must be able to camouflage their vehicles and campsites. They must also be able to navigate by the stars, since they often move during the night to avoid detection and because it is cooler. Since the Light Strike Vehicles can only carry a 500–600kg payload and the load the Land Rovers can carry is finite, Mobility Troop must either have caches of water, food, and fuel or be resupplied via airdrop. Each troop member will need up to nine liters of water per day in the desert, making it necessary to either know of sources of water, which will frequently be controlled by the enemy, or have caches or resupply drops.

The romantic ties with the old SAS of the desert often make Mobility Troop especially appealing to veterans of the Regiment who show up for Remembrance Day ceremonies. Like any

other members of the SAS, the men of Mobility Troop fight where they're sent and learn whatever new skills are needed. If it's the desert, they'll take the lead, but if it's another environment, they'll follow the other specialists who are trained and equipped for it.

Those assigned to an SAS Mountain Troop specialize in cold weather and high-altitude warfare. They combine the skills of mountaineering, skiing, and Arctic operations necessary for troops to fight in the hostile terrain and temperatures likely to be encountered in such far-off battlefields as the Falklands and Norway. The basic elements of Arctic or mountain operations are survival, mobility, and capability. SAS Mountain specialists, therefore, learn the skills that enable them to master each of these elements.

They are taught these basics in Arctic survival training, normally in Norway, as well as how to bring in aerial resupply in mountainous or snowy regions. Specifically, they learn how to build snow caves and igloos, choose properly layered clothing for warmth, build and maintain fires, acquire fuel (the SAS Operations Research Unit has done research on using human feces as fuel in cold climates and also in desert environments), obtain food through such methods as ice fishing, and get potable water in cold climates, while expending minimal energy.

Along with their survival skills, mountain specialists learn different ways to be mobile in their operational environments, one of the first being how to make parachute jumps into the snow. Skiing is an especially important skill since movement rate is more than doubled on skis and energy use is more than halved. Trained ski troops in an Arctic environment should be able to move at the rate of 4km per hour cross country with full equipment; SAS Mountain Troop members normally meet or exceed this rate and should be able to cover 40–50km per day with at least 100lb of equipment. To haul heavier equipment and supplies, they use small sledges. Snowshoeing is another alternative, especially in soft snow, and for extended cross-country skiing operations, there is ski-joring, a technique in which skiers are

The famous SAS Pink Panther. Special Air Service

towed behind cross-country vehicles. In addition to mastering these techniques, SAS Mountain Troop members learn to drive the various types of snowcats, snowmobiles, and other specialized vehicles. For situations involving an entire SAS Squadron or when the Mountain Troop may be acting as scouts for a larger formation, Mountain Troop members learn to cut a trail through the snow for troops less experienced in Arctic operations by using a breaker, two cutters, and packers. They also learn Alpine techniques, including rock climbing, rappelling, and belaying, as well as specialized "mountain walking," where they step over obstacles that could cause avalanches or could fall. Traditional "commando" skills such as climbing rope bridges are reinforced during this training, too.

The entire purpose of placing an SAS soldier in a hostile environment is so that he can fight; therefore, the troops maintain combat readiness. One of the most important lessons Mountain and Arctic Troops must learn is to properly maintain their weapons so that they will function in cold weather. Residual oil can freeze and must be removed. They also hone their specialized marksmanship skills, such as using crossed ski poles as a shooting rest, shooting from skis and then rapidly moving away cross country, and preparing ambushes from snow caves. Due to the likelihood of longer-

39

Among the various units that have copied the famed SAS Pink Panthers are the Spanish Foreign Legion, which developed specialized four-wheel-drive vehicles *for their Special Operations Unit.* Spanish Foreign Legion

range shots, especially in the mountains, a substantial number of Mountain Troop members will qualify as snipers.

Attendance at other specialized schools, such as the British or German Mountain Leader schools, or the US Ranger course, and cross training with units such as the German Gebirgsjaeger and Italy's Alpini help SAS Mountain Troop members develop their basic mountaineering and skiing skills even further while becoming familiar with the tactics used by other

troops specializing in their area of operations.

All troops receive intensive jungle training. Only about twenty percent of the world's land surface is tropical, but during the last half-century, this small area has been home to most of the world's insurgencies. The "ulu," as the SAS refers to the jungle, can be both friend and enemy, and SAS jungle training is designed to allow soldiers to operate successfully for extended periods in this environment. One SAS patrol in Malaya, for example, spent 103 consecutive days deep in the jungle. Spencer Chapman titled his classic work on jungle warfare *The Jungle is Neutral*, but the SAS attempts to move past that neutrality and turn the jungle into an ally.

In Malaya, for example, the jungle canopy was so thick that parachute insertions seemed impossible; however, the SAS developed the technique of tree-jumping, in which parachutists descended into the treetops and then used specially designed harnesses to lower themselves to the ground. In Borneo, where the SAS operated border surveillance posts, they adapted their substantial camouflage skills to blend into the jungle.

The basic rules of camouflage as practiced by the SAS are that regardless of the environment, the following have to be hidden: shape, shine, silhouette, sound, smell, color, and association. To break up the shape of a soldier, for example, rifles, packs, and headgear will normally have to be obscured. A combination of camouflage tape, headbands or flop hats, and local flora threaded into equipment can help change the distinctive shape. Any shiny metallic surfaces should be taped or wound with camouflage, and camouflage cream can obscure faces and hands. Avoiding detection through silhouette is mostly a matter of discipline, so that the soldier avoids standing up on ridgelines or against light sources. Soundlessness in the jungle or other environments is once again a matter of discipline and practice. Patrols will often give themselves the "jump test" before moving into an operational area, jumping up and down to see if any equipment needs to be taped to prevent sound. Smell may be camouflaged either by not bathing so that no soap smell is present or by bathing with the most neutral soap possible so that there is no body smell. Color camouflage is mostly a matter of avoiding highly visible colors that clash with the natural environment. Avoiding association can include such simple techniques as making sure that any remaining footprints do not look like British Army boots. In Borneo, for example, SAS soldiers altered the cleat pattern on their boots to resemble Indonesian issue ones. US MACV/SOG personnel in Vietnam went one better, testing jungle boots

with the soles molded to resemble small Vietnamese bare feet. These proved so uncomfortable that they were never adopted.

Soldiers must learn to deal with the jungle heat by choosing appropriate clothing and with moisture by maintaining careful hygiene to avoid fungus infections. Weapons must be carefully maintained in this humid environment also, to avoid rust. Ironically, despite the prevalence of moisture, safe drinking water can be scarce. SAS practice is normally to filter the water in a Millbank bag and then use water purification tablets. Insects and diseases are often more dangerous than a human enemy, and maintaining the ability to fight after moving through the debilitating swamps likely to be encountered takes constant attention. Much of learning to navigate, survive, and fight in the jungle is acclimatization, which is why the SAS puts such stress on jungle training. Adding to navigational difficulty in the jungle is the frequent presence of fog.

Shelter is usually not a problem, but if operations are conducted during the monsoon, the constant rain will destroy most short-term shelters. Bamboo, Atap, palm, and rattan are all useful for building shelter and are all readily available. Waterways often offer the fastest means of transport, but since the jungle normally comes right to the shoreline, it is also very easy to be ambushed while moving on a river or stream.

Patrol specialists have to adapt their special skills to the jungle, whether it is the explosives expert who must determine how to blow a landing zone for a helicopter evacuation or the medic who must combat disease and infection likely to be encountered. Troop skills may also be adapted to the jungle environment, especially in the case of Boat Troop, which can use their Kleppers or Geminis to move through jungle waterways, or HALO Troop which might still have to use tree-jumping techniques.

Other specialties will be learned by selected members of the SAS. Counterterrorism, or Counter Revolutionary Warfare as the SAS terms it, is considered a skill much like jungle warfare and one that every member of the SAS

should be familiar with. Intelligence gathering is considered a standard SAS skill, but intelligence analysis and interpretation falls to the SAS Operational Intelligence Unit, known in the Regiment as "The Kremlin." Staffed primarily by senior noncommissioned officers, the Operational Intelligence Unit has access to signals intelligence, satellite imagery, agent reports, and other materials from MI6 (more officially known as the Secret Intelligence Service) and friendly intelligence agencies. The SAS Operational Intelligence Unit works especially closely with other friendly special operations intelligence personnel, such as those from US Special Forces Delta. Emphasis within SAS intelligence is placed on information that might prove useful to Sabre Squadrons deployed on missions. Prospective areas of operations are given intense scrutiny and a database is compiled, listing their geography, climate, political structure, government, economy, security forces, and alliances. Computers now compile pertinent information which might prove necessary for a night parachute jump or an underwater landing virtually anywhere in the world. Within the Operations Intelligence Unit will be specialists on terrain, counterinsurgency, explosives, terrorism, psychological profiling, and languages. Many standard SAS skills will prove invaluable here. The SAS retains close ties with MI5 (officially the Security Service) and MI6, often acting as the "teeth" for one of the intelligence services. Operations Intelligence also maintains close ties with GCHQ, the British equivalent of the National Security Agency. In addition to its own highly trained signalers, 22nd SAS can draw on the specialists of 264 (SAS) Signals, an airborne-qualified unit assigned to support the Regiment, for help with radio intercept and security.

Another specialist skill is sniping. As a skilled sniper, the SAS soldier can not only prove invaluable in counterterrorist operations but exert an effect far out of proportion by demoralizing and tying down the enemy. Should an SAS patrol be assigned to carry out a surgical assassination of a high-ranking enemy officer or a terrorist leader, sniping skills may prove invaluable. Selectively killing officers, radio operators, or weapons crews can severely erode the efficiency of much larger units, too. Members of the SAS deemed good candidates for sniper training may attend the British Army's four-week sniper course or the even-tougher Royal Marine six-week course. SAS soldiers have also attended Allied sniper courses such as the US Marine Corps one. Some skills the SAS soldier already possesses are enhanced in sniper training, including building hides, stalking, range estimation, camouflage, observation, and of course, marksmanship out to at least 600m. Different variations of the Accuracy International PM rifle are used, depending on the mission. For standard military operations, the 7.62mm NATO infantry model with Schmidt & Bender 6X telescopic sight is normally chosen, although the "moderated" (silenced) version may be used. For counterterrorist duties, either the 7.62mm NATO or the .243 CT version with Schmidt & Bender 12X scope may be chosen; the choice for especially long shots is the .300 Winchester Magnum long-range version.

SAS training is designed to make each soldier a well-trained individual as well as a cog in the SAS machine whose skills mesh with those of the rest of the patrol and troop. Since long-service NCOs learn additional patrol and troop skills throughout their careers and receive other specialized training, even a small number of SAS soldiers normally can display an amazing versatility in the types of missions they can undertake. Perhaps one of the greatest strengths of the SAS has been its ability to create an elite group of versatile specialists!

SAS Mountain and Arctic Warfare Troop members are highly skilled skiers; most long-serving members of the SAS have received some ski training.

Chapter 3

Desert Warriors

More than two years before David Stirling's fertile mind conceived of the SAS while lying in a hospital bed, Major Ralph Bagnold had suggested the formation of a long-range desert reconnaissance force. The result would be the Long-Range Desert Group (LRDG), which came into existence after Italy's declaration of war against Great Britain on June 10, 1940. Suddenly, General Sir Alexandria Wavell needed intelligence from Libya—and needed it quickly. This first reconnaissance into the Great Sand Sea by what was known at that point as the Long-Range Patrol Unit took thirteen days and gave Wavell first-hand intelligence to the effect that Italy did not appear to be preparing an offensive. October 1940 saw the arrival of Orde Wingate in the Middle East. Wingate immediately suggested the formation of a large force to operate in the enemy rear, a force that would be resupplied by air. This forerunner of Wingate's later Chindits never materialized, but it did cause substantial interest in operations behind the lines in the Middle East.

Building on a combination of his original concept and Wingate's ideas, Bagnold suggested a modified plan calling for a force to carry out reconnaissance and harassment as well as to cooperate with the Free French in removing Arab support for the Italians. Eventually, Bagnold foresaw a raiding unit with its own mobile artillery and light armor as well as close air support, all capable of combining for a mission behind Italian lines and then dispersing. Ground Headquarters could not spare the resources in equipment or manpower to fully implement Bagnold's plan, but he was permitted to form a small artillery and armored contingent and to begin trials of the 10 Ton Truck for desert operations. Beginning late in 1941 and continuing for the next two-and-one-half years, there would be an LRDG patrol operating somewhere in the enemy rear virtually at all times.

From the beginning, it became obvious that personnel selected for the LRDG would have to be a special type of soldier: self-reliant, adaptable, able to operate in small isolated groups for extended periods, and skilled at driving and vehicle repairs, radio operation, weapons, and land navigation. Many of the earliest members were from Rhodesia, New Zealand, and Australia. There were also many volunteers from British regiments, but the fact that a higher percentage of Commonwealth soldiers had owned and maintained vehicles worked in their favor. There was, in fact, a long waiting list to join the LRDG and very rarely were trainees returned to their units as unsuitable.

As initially formed the Long Range Patrol Unit had a headquarters and three patrols, each with two officers, twenty-eight operational researchers, and four reinforcements. Eleven vehicles transported a patrol. Experience soon

Many of the founding members of the SAS received their initial close-combat training from W. E. Fairbairn at the Commando Training Center. Dorothea Fairbairn

45

showed that a patrol operated most effectively when split in half, so in the fall of 1941, a patrol was re-organized into two half-patrols, each with one officer and fifteen to twenty other ranks carried in five or six vehicles. Each half-patrol could be broken into two troops. For example, in the fall 1941, the LRDG consisted of Signal, Air, Survey, and Heavy Sections plus the A Squadron with three patrols and the B Squadron with two patrols. Each of the five patrols was organized as follows: first half-patrol—a Chevrolet 1500lb pilot car with the commanding officer, a Ford 3000lb truck with radio and navigation equipment and operators, a Ford 3000lb truck with the patrol sergeant, a Ford 3000lb truck with the medic, and a Ford 3000lb truck with the mechanic; second half-patrol—a Ford 3000lb truck with the commanding officer, a Ford 3000lb truck with radio and navigation equipment and operators, a Ford 3000lb truck with the patrol sergeant, a Ford 3000lb truck with the medic, and a Ford 3000lb truck with the mechanic. A Ford 3000lb truck with a Bofors 37mm antitank gun mounted was attached to whichever half-patrol needed the heavier armament for its mission. Other vehicles—extra radio trucks, for example—could be drawn as needed for missions. At this stage, 4x4 Fords were being used, but in March 1942, special Canadian Chevrolet 1533X2 4x2 trucks with open cabs were in service. These trucks were fitted out much like the later SAS desert vehicles, and 20mm Breda guns replaced the Bofors. Armament for each patrol initially included ten Lewis guns, four Boys antitank rifles, and the Bofors. One Vickers was soon tried as a replacement for a Lewis gun and proved so effective in the antiaircraft role that the mix was soon seven Lewis guns and three Vickers. Patrols also carried 2in mortars.

By March 1942, the LRDG would grow to twenty-five officers and 324 other ranks with 110 vehicles. Reflecting the stress on keeping the vehicles running and on communications, thirty-six ORs were signals personnel and thirty-six were mechanics. The signalers were especially important, as the LRDG had to be able to communicate over long distances despite bad atmospheric conditions in the desert. Eventually, the LRDG would be able to draw radio operators from the Irregular Warfare Operators School, which trained SOE and other clandestine operators. This made good sense, as the LRDG worked closely with the Secret Intelligence Service (MI6), MI9 (which set up escape and evasion routes), clandestine sabotage teams, Popski's Private Army, and later, the SAS and Special Boat Service. Their special skills soon made the LRDG the jacks-of-all-trades behind Axis lines.

Many of the precepts developed by the LRDG have in the last half-century become standard operating procedure for special operations units. For example, the LRDG discovered that intelligence operations and offensive operations should be separated, as the former could be carried out effectively only if the enemy was not aware of the LRDG's presence. As a result, one standard operating procedure was that attacks could be made against targets of opportunity only on the way back from an intelligence-gathering mission. Later SAS raids were planned away from LRDG surveillance sites. Highly effective camouflage was developed to avoid detection from the air. Because they were operating far from medical help, the LRDG's medics had become competent at dealing with diverse injuries on their own. To prevent all key personnel from being wiped out, the patrol commander and second in command traveled in separate vehicles, as did navigators and signalers. When patrols were on missions requiring less fuel or water than usual, they cached these necessities for later usage. Later in the war, the LRDG would also act as forward air controllers to call in air strikes on promising enemy targets.

LRDG missions were primarily reconnaissance to gather intelligence and route information for other units, with agent escort or courier work for various clandestine agencies and attacks on enemy transport and communication secondary. As respect for their abilities increased, so did the diversity of their missions. Whatever else they were doing, however, the LRDG gathered intelligence about enemy move-

Silent killing technique at the Commando Training Center. IWM

ments and accumulated topographical information that played a key role in every major British offensive. LRDG road watches also kept Ground Headquarters extremely well-informed about enemy supplies and movement and aided in developing intelligence estimates about German Field Marshall Erwin Rommel's intent. LRDG information, in fact, fit extremely well with "Ultra" intercepts to give British intelligence a glance into the enemy's supply difficulties. Similar to later US Special Forces "Eldest Son" operations in Vietnam, LRDG units also planted cases of Italian ammunition which had been rigged to explode and aided "A Force" in other deceptions, including allowing fake offen-

sive plans to be captured. Because the LRDG was able to make surveys, Army cartographers were able to produce accurate maps showing oases and other important features.

So good were the LRDG units at navigation that they often acted as pathfinders for other units, including special operations ones such as the Middle East Commandos. Similar to their pathfinder duties were their assignments as couriers or delivery services for nearly 100 intelligence agents during their operations in the Western Desert. In addition to deliveries, the LRDG also made pickups—of agents, downed airmen, and escaped Allied prisoners. Although the SAS would make the hit-and-run raid from the desert an art form, the LRDG had proven to be quite effective at various types of raids. Raids on Axis mail, laying mines deep behind the lines, attacks on tanker trucks, and blowing up supply dumps all fell within the LRDG purview. Later, they often operated in conjunction with the SAS, initially as pathfinders and later as co-raiders. There is little doubt, however, that members of today's Mobility Troops would have fit into the LRDG quite well.

Although they would later work together with excellent results and their exploits are often confused, the genesis for the SAS was not with the LRDG, however. David Stirling was a Scots Guards officer out of Cambridge who was attracted by the special forces idea and transferred to no. 8 Commando. Then, assigned to "Layforce," he arrived in the Middle East. While in the Middle East, Stirling taught himself to parachute, in the process injuring his back, resulting in temporary paralysis. While recuperating, he developed plans for a unit to raid Rommel's logistics network and air power. Stirling's basic precepts were that the Axis forces were vulnerable to attacks on transport; large com-

Silent killing with the knife, here being taught to a member of the French Commandos; the same carotid thrust was taught to the SAS. IWM

mando raids involving up to 200 men lost the element of surprise, whereas with surprise on its side, a five-man raiding party could destroy as much as a 200-man raiding party; and a small raiding force could be inserted by parachute, small boat, Jeep, or other means. Before fully recovered, he then "infiltrated" General Auchinleck's headquarters on crutches to present his plan. Promoted to captain and given permission to raise an airborne/commando unit known as "L Detachment" for desert raiding, Stirling initially was allowed to raise five officers and sixty other ranks from "Layforce." Among his early recruits was "Paddy" Mayne, soon to become a legendary founder of the SAS, but then in trouble for striking his commanding officer. Many of the other "originals," as they would later be known, did not fit into conventional military units much better. Stirling's conception of the SAS as a meritocracy, where the emphasis was on excellence and class distinctions were ignored, drew many rugged individualists such as Mayne to the SAS.

At this point, the LRDG was designated as the parent organization for the SAS, to give logistical support. Although he had initially suggested five-man patrols, Stirling soon settled on the four-man patrol for the basic SAS operational unit. Initial training reflected the SAS's willingness to adopt unconventional methods. With no jump towers or captive balloons available, for example, the fledgling SAS members practiced landings by rolling off of a truck traveling 30mph. This was later "improved" upon by using a sled from which trainees rolled off as it sped down an incline. Other skills were similar to those found necessary by the LRDG: medicine, intelligence gathering, demolitions, and communications. Swimming, desert marches, German and Italian weapons familiarization, and desert navigation filled out the training over the next months. They learned their infiltration skills well, demonstrating their operational readiness by infiltrating an RAF base, planting dummy bombs on the aircraft, and then fading back into the desert. One of the first lessons the SAS learned in training was the need for a lightweight yet powerful explosive device. With none available, Jock Lewes, who Stirling had placed in charge of training, invented one—helping to establish the SAS tradition of inventing what was needed if it wasn't available in military stores. Lewes is also credited with designing the distinctive SAS parachute wing.

The initial SAS raid was not as successful. On May 6, 1941, Stirling led his men on their first raid as they jumped behind enemy lines to launch a series of airfield attacks. Their inexperience at parachute operations combined with a blowing sandstorm caused the drop to be widely dispersed, however, and Stirling and twenty-one of his men were lucky to make it back to the LRDG rendezvous points.

As the Afrikakorps successfully pushed back the 8th Army, however, the SAS soon got another chance to prove itself. In December, the LRDG inserted Stirling's raiders for another airfield raid, this one highly successful. At Tamit, Paddy Mayne and his group destroyed twenty-four aircraft as well as bomb and gasoline dumps. Bill Fraser's group had done even better at Agedabia, where they destroyed thirty-seven aircraft. At the two airfields, sixty-one aircraft were destroyed. Now on the offensive, the 8th Army launched another raid almost immediately, Mayne's group destroying twenty-seven more. So successful did the SAS become at this type of raid that it was often said there were more "aces" in the SAS than the Desert Air Force. These early raids were not without losses, however. Jock Lewes was among those lost to enemy air attacks on LRDG trucks picking up the raiders. These air attacks prevented another group under Bill Fraser from being rescued. With virtually no water and hundreds of miles of desert to traverse on foot, they walked most of the way and stole enemy transport to cover the rest. Such feats helped establish the mystique of the SAS.

These early successes had gained attention for the SAS and assured its continued existence. Auchinleck, in fact, gave Stirling permission to recruit another six officers and forty other ranks and promoted him to the rank of major. With the Afrikakorps in retreat, Stirling was also looking for ways to harass the "Desert Fox's"

supply lines and raid the port of Bouerat to prevent Rommel from using it. Among the new additions to the SAS were a group of Free French paratroopers. He also added two members of the Special Boat Section whose skills were deemed useful in raiding the port of Bouerat.

Stirling led this raid himself, with Paddy Mayne now unhappily in charge of training new recruits. After being delivered within sixty miles of the target by the LRDG, sixteen SAS/SBS and four LRDG members piled into one truck for the final approach to the target. They successfully destroyed the port facilities, but the mission proved unnecessary, as Rommel had retaken the much larger port of Benghazi. As the patrol returned, in fact, they found the 8th Army in retreat and the LRDG forward base at Jalo evacuated. When they did make it back to Kabrit in early February, however, Stirling was pleased to find that the French SAS members were ready to go operational. The next good raiding period of moonless nights would not be until March, so Stirling began planning a series of raids on airfields around Benghazi and on the harbor itself.

With the 8th Army dug in along the Gazala Line and on the defensive, operations against Rommel's supply lines, especially if they could disrupt arrivals at Benghazi, were considered highly desirable. As a result, on March 15, 1942, Stirling set off for Benghazi with all of L Detachment. Stirling himself was in the first of the SAS's special raiding vehicles, his "Blitz buggy." From a camp in the Jebel Mountains near Benghazi, Stirling, three other members of the SAS, and two SBS men loaded into the "Blitz Buggy" and drove into Benghazi at night and directly to the waterfront without being challenged. They scouted the area but withdrew without placing explosives. The airfield attacks by other parties were not especially successful, although as usual Paddy Mayne's group did well, destroying fifteen German aircraft. The other groups destroyed only one aircraft between them.

Nevertheless, when they returned to Kabrit, they were considered enough of a drain on Rommel's aircraft and manpower that sufficient new troops were allotted for the formation of a second troop. Stirling was already planning to go back to Benghazi to destroy harbor shipping. As a result, he acquired some inflatable boats and practiced placing dummy limpet mines on Allied shipping at Port Suez. Stirling launched his next attack on Benghazi in mid-May. His group included Prime Minister Winston Churchill's son Randolph and Fitzroy Maclean, a member of Parliament. They traveled in the Blitz Buggy, tagging along with an LRDG patrol.

Once again, the raiders drove audaciously into the town of Benghazi, hiding the Blitz Buggy in a deserted garage across from the German headquarters. Then, carrying their boats and explosives, they walked directly onto the docks, but discovered that both boats were defective and would not inflate. An extremely frustrated Stirling had to abort an attack on the ships in the harbor a second time. Rather than skulking back to their garage, however, they walked directly by the sentries guarding the port, taking time for Fitzroy Maclean to fluently berate them for not standing better guard. Once back at the garage, they decided to hold up through the next day, although in the afternoon Stirling got bored and, putting on sunglasses as a "disguise," took a stroll around the docks. They left that night without setting any explosive charges, feeling it was better not to call attention to the lax defenses in case they wanted to come back. The two forays into Benghazi, although not successful in destroying shipping, certainly showed the daring that would become the SAS's trademark.

After the return from Benghazi, Stirling, driving as wildly as he did when raiding German airfields, was in an accident in which Maclean was injured badly enough to spend three months in the hospital and Churchill badly enough to be invalided back to Great Britain. While planning new raids, Stirling had to contend with staff officers who wanted to assign the SAS to a larger parachute formation, where it would be used in the tactical role in support of other operations. Stirling continued to fight, however, for the SAS's position as a strategic

unit intended to launch raids in support of overall 8th Army objectives.

Feeling the need to graphically illustrate SAS capabilities, Stirling wanted to hit the most important airfields in Libya, Cyrenaica, Crete, Rhodes, and Greece. He selected a total of thirty targets to be attacked by 120–160 men. In his attempts to draw special operations forces from throughout North Africa under his auspices, Stirling had added the Special Interrogation Group, which was composed of German-speaking Palestinian Jews (some of whom had served in the German Army), German-speaking British soldiers, and a few turncoats from the Afrikakorps. Just as the Middle East Commando had been formed to carry out the type of raids the various commandos had launched against the coasts of Europe, the Special Interrogation Group was seen as a Middle East equivalent of X Troop of no. 10 (Inter-Allied Commando). Composed of German speakers, X Troop was often used for infiltration raids where their specialized language skills were necessary.

With the Luftwaffe pounding Malta, Auchinleck was ordered to go on the offensive to take some of the pressure off the beleaguered island. In support, Stirling volunteered to carry out a series of raids on the night of June 13 against airfields where many of the bombers hitting the Malta convoys were based, although not all of the targets Stirling had designated earlier could be handled with the manpower available.

Three raiding parties left with the LRDG; Stirling and Mayne each led one, and Lieutenant Zirnheld of the Free French led a French party. In a reverse of their normal results, Stirling carried out a successful raid on Benina, while Mayne's attack on Berka Satellite Field was compromised when sentries, now far more alert to possible SAS raids, spotted his party as it approached. The Free French were also spotted at the main Berka Airfield, but still managed to destroy eleven aircraft. Stirling and Mayne withdrew but, at least partially out of competition with each other, then borrowed an LRDG truck and with five others went back to shoot up what transport they could along the roads around the airfields. An accompanying member of the Special Interrogation Group talked their way past roadblocks. They were highly successful in shooting up enemy transport, but while escaping, managed to ignite one of their own time pencils and had to abandon their truck just before it exploded. As a result, they had to walk back to their rendezvous, probably an easier task than explaining the loss of the truck to their LRDG escorts.

Other SAS parties had gone after other targets. A Free French party successfully blew up ammunition dumps at Barce, while other members of the French SAS along with members of the Special Interrogation Group went after Derra and Martuba Airfields. Betrayed by one of the Afrikakorps turncoats, all but two members of these parties were captured. Still another group under Captain the Earl Jellicoe (whose father had commanded the British fleet at Jutland) set out to raid Crete, destroying twenty-one aircraft, primarily Ju 88s that had been pounding Malta. Only Jellicoe and a Greek guide escaped.

While almost everyone else in Cairo worried about Rommel's nearness, Stirling decided that the Germans' overstretched supply lines made them especially vulnerable to raids by such units as the SAS. The resulting decision was that in early July, raids would be launched against the former RAF airfields at Mersa Matruch and Fuka now being used by the Germans. For these raids, the SAS acquired some Jeeps and three-ton Ford trucks. The Jeeps underwent extensive alteration, with two Vickers K machine guns mounted front and rear (in some cases, a single Browning .50 MG replaced one pair of Vickers), suspensions beefed up, an extra fuel tank and water condenser added, and steel sand channels carried. The ancestor of the "Pink Panther" had been born.

At this point, L Detachment could muster about 100 men from its diverse components. Stirling's plan was to move into the desert with them if Cairo fell and carry on a guerrilla war. On July 3, they left for the desert in thirty-five vehicles, three days later rendezvousing with an

As many members of the SAS originally came from the Commandos, they had learned the various Commando scaling and crossing techniques. IWM

LRDG patrol. Six raids were planned for the next night in conjunction with an 8th Army offensive. Stirling and Mayne led the assault on Bagoush Airfield, using a tactic for which they would become famous: Roaring down the runways with machine guns blazing, they left substantial destruction in their wake, although it was questionable whether their previous stealthy entries didn't really incapacitate more aircraft. On the other hand, the Germans and Italians were now on the alert for such infiltrations, as some of the other parties discovered when they attempted their raids on the same night. Although the new tactic was developed at least partially out of Stirling's and Mayne's love

51

of wild adventure, it did allow an SAS raiding party to roar in, inflict substantial damage, and roar out before the enemy could form an organized resistance.

Another raid was launched on the night of July 11, this one carried out by five parties led by Martin, Jellicoe, Jordan, Fraser, and Mayne. They destroyed only twenty-two aircraft, not even up to Mayne's normal standards. After two weeks in the desert, however, the 100 or so raiders were beginning to run short of supplies and fuel, and had to halt operations and send trucks for more supplies. As the Germans now controlled the route north of the Qattara Depression, it was necessary to send the resupply convoy along a route through the supposedly impassable Depression scouted by the LRDG. After picking up supplies and new vehicles at Kabrit, the SAS immediately returned to the desert to join those who had remained behind.

Their next target was the heavily used airfield at Sidi Haneish, which Stirling planned to overwhelm with eighteen Jeeps in two columns. Along with this attack, a diversionary raid would also be launched against Bagoush Airfield. Stirling would lead the entire formation against Sidi Haneish, while Mayne and Jellicoe would each lead one of the Jeep columns. As they roared onto the airfield, which had just been illuminated for landing bombers, both columns fired outward, inflicting damage on parked Heinkels and Junkers, hangers, vehicles, and personnel. After delivering a hail of bullets against the airfield, the Jeeps then sped away and split up to reach the rendezvous separately. The attack certainly proved that despite increased security on German and Italian airfields, the SAS could still inflict heavy damage; forty aircraft were destroyed, including many of the invaluable Ju 52s Rommel used for supply runs. During the actual raid, two Jeeps were lost and one SAS member was killed, and on the way to the rendezvous, Zirnheld of the Free

David Stirling with some of the SAS parties that caused havoc behind German lines in the Western Desert. IWM

53

French was killed in an attack by a German aircraft.

Despite his success, Stirling was so disgusted with the lack of support he was receiving from 8th Army at this point that he suggested placing the SAS under the RAF so that he could be sure of aerial resupply. Middle East Headquarters, however, ordered Stirling home to plan new operations. These new operations included Benghazzi, the site of Stirling's two earlier "visits," as well as Tobruk, both important harbors for supplying the Afrikakorps. To give Stirling the additional manpower he needed, members of the 1st Special Service Regiment were assigned to the SAS, even though they had not received specialized desert training. The LRDG was assigned to raid Barce Airfield, while the Sudan Defense Force would retake Jalo Oasis to secure the SAS's return route.

As the plan evolved, it called for 200 men in forty Jeeps plus forty supply trucks. The sheer numbers began to resemble those of the personnel-heavy Commando operations. Stirling's vision was of an organization that could carry out such plans more economically and effectively. While this raid was being planned, Stirling dined with Winston Churchill, who was visiting North Africa. Explaining his vision of the SAS, Stirling proved adept at fighting a bureaucratic guerrilla war behind the lines of Middle East Headquarters. Churchill, who always identified with the special raiding forces, promised Stirling his support.

Modifying new Jeeps, training new recruits, and stockpiling supplies continued through August. Once the SAS was ready to launch its attack, it formed three convoys—involving 231 men in forty-five Jeeps plus almost as many supply trucks and two tanks, assigned to break through roadblocks—something Stirling's Jeep Patrols did successfully, using speed, surprise, and firepower. The three convoys arrived at Kufra Oasis, their jumping-off point. The Benghazzi assault unit was divided into three parties, which began leaving on September 4 to cross the Great Sand Sea. They rendezvoused in the mountains again on September 9 and 10, but had to leave their tanks behind mired in the

sand. The raid against Benghazzi was launched on September 13, but the Germans were waiting and little damage was done. Over the next few days, the raiding parties faced constant attacks by German aircraft, losing forty-five vehicles, as well as six killed, eighteen wounded, and five missing. The survivors withdrew to Jalo, then to Kufra. The Tobruk raid was, if anything, an even bigger disaster, with most of those involved becoming casualties. The one bright note was that the LRDG attack on Barce destroyed fifteen aircraft.

While reorganizing the survivors, Stirling was promoted to lieutenant colonel and given command of the newly formed 1st SAS Regiment. With a Headquarters Squadron, plus A, B, C (Free French), and D (SBS) Squadrons, the new unit when fully operational would be able to undertake multiple operations at one time. Each squadron was organized into three troops, each with three sections. The Headquarters Squad-ron included specialists such as a Depot Troop, Intelligence Troop, Signals Troop, Parachute-training Troop, and a Light-repair Section. The fully staffed SAS Regiment would have slots for twenty-nine officers and 572 other ranks.

British Field Marshall Bernard Montgomery was the new commander of the 8th Army, and in an attempt to regain the offensive, made plans to attack El Alamein in early November. To continue to harass Rommel's supply lines, thus weakening German front-line units, A Squadron under Paddy Mayne in late September was ordered to begin carrying out raids immediately against roadways, rail lines, ammunition and fuel dumps, and road transport. As most of the experienced personnel were now concentrated in A Squadron, this did not prove too difficult. Once the battle had been won and Rommel's forces were in retreat, A Squadron would then begin to harass them. During the last three weeks before the El Alamein offensive began, Mayne's raiders had managed to shut down the railway for thirteen of the twenty-one days. By the end of October, Mayne had been ordered to concentrate on fuel supplies in an attempt to inhibit Rommel's ability to maneuver.

The 8th Army rolled over the Afrikakorps, and Mayne's A Squadron successfully harassed their retreat through the end of November.

At about this point, Stirling, realizing that the battle for North Africa was about over, began looking ahead to how the SAS might be gainfully employed. He planned to send Mayne's men to Lebanon for ski training when they returned, while other squadrons would receive small boat training, although presumably D Squadron would not need much more than refresher training. Operations against the Germans continued, though. By mid-December, B Squadron was also operational. Functioning primarily with eight, three-Jeep Patrols, B Squadron suffered quite heavy casualties, mostly among the inexperienced personnel.

The last SAS operations in North Africa were intended to aid the 8th Army's attack on Tripoli. Stirling saw four main objectives: to create a distraction west of Tripoli, to raid German convoys just east of the Port of Gabes, to recce the Mareth Line, where the Germans had occupied French-entrenched positions, and to personally lead a patrol to link up with the 1st Army advancing from Algeria. In trying to make it through the German lines, however, Stirling was captured. He would spend the remainder of the war as a prisoner of the Germans at Colditz. Although the SAS would carry out many successful behind-the-lines operations in Europe and the SBS would be widely used in the Mediterranean, Aegean, and Adriatic, the loss of Stirling removed the SAS's direct line to higher authority and allowed the unit to be absorbed as part of other parachute or raiding formations—a fate Stirling had fought against from the beginning.

Although in its later stages not part of the war in the desert, SBS operations in the Mediterranean need to be mentioned here, as they evolved from Stirling's raiders and were the forerunners of today's Boat Troops. The original Special Boat Section was comprised of commandos who had been trained in the folboat, a canoe made of rubberized canvas on a wooden frame and easily dismantled for transport. Lieutenant Roger Courtney had trained the original unit on the west coast of Scotland. In February 1941, after receiving training with no. 8 Commando, seventeen SBS members were sent to the Middle East, where they were eventually incorporated into Stirling's command more than a year later. Another SBS unit—101 Troop—was later formed at Dover and, after assignment to no. 6 Commando, used on cross-channel raids, such as a highly successful one in April 1942 on Boulogne Harbor. The SBS also worked with COPPs (Combined Operations Assault Pilotage Parties), combat swimmers trained to survey beaches and another forerunner of today's Boat Troop SCUBA experts.

By the end of 1942, fifty-five SBS troops were serving with the SAS. In April 1943, after Stirling's capture, 250 B Squadron members, including the former SBS men, became the Special Boat Squadron of the SAS under Major the Earl Jellicoe. Each of three SBS detachments contained six patrols of thirteen men each. Each detachment was designated by the letter of its commanding officer's last name: L for Langton, M for Maclean, and S for Sutherland. Now based near Haifa, the SBS began training with the Greek Sacred Squadron, an elite raiding unit comprised of former Greek officers (Anthony Quinn's character in *The Guns of Navarone* was a member of the Sacred Squadron). The mission of these two units was to raid islands in the Mediterranean and Aegean Seas.

In June 1943, for example, more than a dozen SBS members—now designated the Special Boat Service—raided Kastelli Airfield on Crete. One four-man patrol on this mission was led by Anders Lassen, a legendary SAS/SBS member who would later win the Victoria Cross. During late 1943, some SBS members helped scout Sicily in preparation for the invasion, but the primary mission remained operations in the Dodecanese Islands. Various islands were at times "conquered" and occupied by the SBS, including Cos, Leros, and Simi. Simi proved an excellent jumping-off point for raids on German bases on Rhodes. In fall 1943, though, the Germans began retaking the islands. The last to fall was Leros, where 600 German paratroopers were dropped. The SBS were parachutists themselves and realized how vulnerable the Germans were right after the drop, especially the Fallschirmjaegers, who jumped with only a pistol until they had recovered their equipment containers with heavier weapons. By sniping at the paratroopers whenever they tried to recover these containers, the SBS men held them off for some time. When Leros was taken, all but one wounded SBS trooper managed to escape, and even he showed true SAS spirit—after being captured, he soon stole a German boat and rowed it to Turkey sixty miles away. So effective was the SBS campaign that by the beginning of 1944, 200–300 SBS soldiers had tied down six German divisions in the Aegean Islands.

From ships in neutral Turkish waters, the SBS continued to launch raids on islands throughout the area. In July 1944, 139 SBS and Sacred Squadron members recaptured Simi, but withdrew before the Germans could launch a full counterattack. This was the last major raid in the Aegean, although SBS members remained to assist the Greek Sacred Squadron. Most SBS operations, however, moved to the Adriatic in the spring 1944. Other non-SAS/SBS units were also operating in Europe and Burma. In April 1944, fourteen SBS soldiers virtually wiped out forty-eight Italians and Germans on Thera, and on July 23, they raided Crete, destroying 165,000gal of gasoline, blowing up trucks and staff cars, and killing thirty-two Germans. The SBS also carried out a few operations in Yugoslavia, but Marshal Josip Tito was distrustful of the British and requested that the SBS not operate in his territory. During the German withdrawal from Greece, sixty SBS men under Major Ian Patterson did manage to bluff 2,500 Germans and Greek collaborators into surrendering at Patras. Sixty SBS men also managed to "liberate" Athens. As the Germans left Greece, the SBS was right behind, harassing them on their way. Other raids during fall 1944 had been carried out against Salonika and Albania, as well as German-held islands in the Adriatic.

To some extent because SBS operations were making the partisans in Yugoslavia look bad, the SBS was pulled out of the Adriatic in

April 1945. On April 9, 1945, however, some of these SBS soldiers participated in a raid at Lake Comacchio, where Anders Lassen's heroism earned him a posthumous Victoria Cross. In the best SAS traditions, the SBS had sewn confusion and destruction among German island garrisons and had tied down many times their own numbers on garrison duty. Whenever possible, they continued to raid airfields, too. They had also established the value of skilled boat handlers among SAS personnel, thus laying the foundation for today's SAS Boat Troops.

Oman

Beginning in 1954, the Beni Hina tribe, with Saudi support, revolted against the Sultan of Oman, a traditional British ally. During the next three years, these insurgents carried out raids against the Sultan's armed forces. As the British-trained Trucial Oman Scouts and other units gained some successes, however, the guerrillas retreated to the Jebel Akhdar, a rugged plateau reachable only by scaling its treacherous cliffs. There, they set up machine guns covering each approach and deployed snipers, venturing out only to conduct raids or plant mines, the latter of which accounted for 150 destroyed vehicles between March and November 1958.

The Sultan of Oman had denied his subjects any benefits of the modern world, including medical treatment, and the British were afraid their support of him might cause criticism in the United Nations. Hence, they wanted to see the rebellion ended as soon as possible, with minimal fanfare.

One plan called for Major Frank Kitson, who had experienced the value of pseudo-guerrillas in Kenya, to form groups of rebels-turned-allies into hunter groups. Before he could implement this plan, however, the SAS was deployed to Oman. D Squadron was operating along the Thai border with Malaya, hunting down remaining Communist guerrillas, when it received orders to prepare to be deployed to Oman. They immediately began polishing their long-range shooting skills. D Squadron arrived in Muscat on November 18, 1958, and almost immediately began carrying out reconnaissance missions to determine possible routes to the top of the Jebel Akhdar. The skillful guerrilla marksman atop the plateau, however, quickly convinced them to patrol at night.

The guerrillas were so confident that the cliffs leading to their stronghold could not be scaled that they didn't plant guards along many approach routes. As a result, thirty D Squadron members climbed 2000m on the north side of the mountain and seized a small foothold on the plateau. With assistance from members of the Life Guards, the SAS would hold this position for the next few weeks and would carry out reconnaissance missions from it. The rebels still really controlled the plateau, however.

Under pressure to quickly resolve the situation in Oman, the British government ordered A Squadron from Malaya. It arrived on January 9, 1959. 22nd SAS's commander, Lieutenant Colonel Anthony Deane-Drummond, flew into Oman to take part in the planning process that would lead to the final SAS assault on the Jebel Akhdar.

As the plan evolved, a diversionary attack would be launched from the "toehold" atop the plateau and another diversion would be launched around the base. Disinformation likely to reach rebel ears had also been planted, indicating a specific route to the top of the cliffs. Members of D Squadron, in concert with a troop of Life Guards, a Signals Detachment, and a machine gun company of the Northern Frontier Force, would actually scale the cliffs in a position left virtually unguarded as a result of the other feints. As dawn approached, however, it appeared quite possible that the assault force would be caught on the cliff face and easily slaughtered. As a result, the SAS troopers left their rucksacks and moved out quickly, carrying only their belt order. One of the first to reach the top was Deane-Drummond himself. As dawn broke and the SAS troops controlled the south side of the plateau, air strikes helped persuade the guerrillas to evacuate the Jebel Akhdar and, thus, effectively broke the rebellion. In addition to returning the SAS to the desert, this short commitment in Oman had also helped assure the continued existence of the SAS as a regular

SAS patrols such as this operated in occupied France and Italy to harry the Axis rear. IWM

regiment that could be used as troubleshooters whenever British interests called for specialist counterinsurgency troops.

Aden

The Federation of South Arabia had been formed in 1959 from six territories on the borders of the Protectorate of Aden, and another ten territories and Aden City would join them over the next four years. Original intent seemed to be that the Federation of South Arabia would remain part of the British Commonwealth, but that was not to be. In 1962, nationalists began waging a guerrilla war against the Federation of South Arabia, with support from Yemen, where Marxist Army officers had toppled the Imam earlier in September. The deposed Imam, however, did not go quietly into exile and was waging his own guerrilla war in the north, with support from Saudi Arabia and at least some ex-SAS mercenaries, against the new leadership in Yemen. This war would last eight years and during the Six-Day War of 1967 would tie down 68,000 Egyptian troops in Yemen. The former SAS members were led by John Cooper, who as a corporal had been Stirling's driver in the Western Desert, and David Smiley, who had been offered command of the regular regiment and two Territorial Army regiments. They were officially mercenaries, but in actuality they were recruited and paid under the auspices of the British government. Even so, there were normally more French than British mercenaries fighting for the Imam. The SAS contingent provided officers, radio operators, and medics.

Two groups were carrying on a guerrilla campaign based in the Radfan Mountains and an urban terrorist campaign in Aden City. The National Liberation Front (NLF) was the more Marxist of the two and received backing from Egypt. The other group was the Front for the Liberation of South Yemen (FLOSY). Despite even more problems than usual from the always-obstreperous tribes in the Radfan Mountains, it was not until December 1963, after a grenade attack on the British High Commissioner, that a state of emergency was finally declared.

Their ruggedness, combined with the searing heat, made the Radfan Mountains an excellent refuge for guerrillas. They were also the funnel for weapons from the Egyptians and Soviets through Yemen. Punitive operations by local government troops had been undertaken with little success, and RAF strikes of the type used to keep the tribesmen in check during the 1920s and 1930s failed. In April 1964 after service in Borneo, the SAS A Squadron arrived in Aden. Since the average SAS soldier is away from home about eight months of the year, deployment immediately for desert training after combat in the jungles of Borneo was not as unusual as it might sound. A Squadron had, in fact, been slated for refresher desert training in Aden; if that training included live-fire operations against NLF and FLOSY, the training would be that much more realistic!

A mixed brigade, including paratroopers and Royal Marine Commandos, had been assigned to secure the Radfan Mountains. The SAS would operate in support of this brigade. Arriving about two weeks before the operation was scheduled to begin—the normal period required to acclimate to the 150deg heat—the SAS launched a combat patrol on the night they arrived. Patrols continued during the next days in preparation for the major move into the Radfan Mountains, scheduled for April 30, 1964. On April 29, an SAS troop preceded the major operation to secure a demilitarized zone for members of the Parachute Regiment who would jump in. Members of the troop were discovered, however, by a goatherd and engaged in an escalating firefight by guerrillas. The SAS soldiers had only eighty rounds each for their rifles and 200 belted rounds each for the Bren gun, and had to conserve their ammunition. They called in air strikes and artillery, but the guerrillas made effective use of the rough terrain and suffered only minor casualties. As dusk approached, the SAS troop's situation grew precarious since they would lose air support. Coordinating their pullout with their artillery support, members of the troop exfiltrated before the area was saturated with artillery fire. Two SAS men were killed before the pullout and had to be left behind; they were later beheaded and their heads displayed in Yemen. During the escape, too, rear security men had to set ambushes to discourage guerrillas from pursuing the troop.

Because the SAS infiltration was compromised, the parachute insertion had to be canceled and the paratroopers and Royal Marines had to spend the next five weeks fighting their way across the Radfan Mountains. A Squadron returned to the United Kingdom a few weeks later, but A, B, and D Squadrons would continue to rotate into Aden for "retraining" as well as doing their tours in Borneo over the next three years.

Of special interest in Aden were what the SAS called "Keeni Meeni" operations (which means "sneaky" in Swahili) in Aden City. These undercover teams were patterned after the "Q" Squads formed by former SAS man Ray Farran with the Palestine police. Fijians and other dark-skinned SAS members who could pass as Arabs were chosen for their appearance and their ability to handle their FN Hi-Power pistols with deadly accuracy and speed. Since the ability to keep their weapon clandestine, yet bring it into action quickly, was so important, they were given intensive drilling with their pistols using the Grant-Taylor close-combat method.

The basic precepts of this training were that a soldier needs surprise, confidence, concentration, speed, and an offensive attitude. It also put stress upon instinctive firing ability. Grant Taylor established three rules: The gun must fit the hand so that it becomes an extension of it; the trigger and hammer must be manipulated skillfully; and the shooter must automatically align the gun on the enemy's kill zone. Among other skills, further instruction worked on firing with either hand, malfunction clearance, two-handed shooting, the "combat crouch," and shooting at multiple targets.

About twenty men were assigned to the Keeni Meeni Squad. Operating in twos or threes, they fanned out through Aden City, looking for the Yemeni-trained assassins who, among other atrocities, had been targeting British school children for grenade attacks. The assassins had also been killing Special Branch officers and their informants, thus depriving security forces of their best sources of intelligence. One effective technique was to send in a lone British soldier in uniform as a stalking horse, who was protected at a distance by Keeni Meenis. Eventually, as SAS squadrons rotated out of Aden, the Keeni Meeni operations were turned over to other regiments trained by the SAS.

In an attempt to stop the arms shipments, the SAS was called upon to mount clandestine patrols and to establish observation posts—both traditional SAS missions. The Radfan Mountains proved to be perfect terrain for good operations, but the heat and difficulty in carrying large quantities of water meant that either the observation posts could be manned for only a short time or they would be compromised when their occupants had to obtain water. Still, SAS observers successfully directed artillery fire onto guerrillas bringing arms across the border or preparing operations against government positions. A few SAS men also worked with local tribal leaders, but a true hearts-and-minds campaign was never launched in Aden.

As the withdrawal of the British Army grew near, SAS patrols were used to carry out reconnaissance to detect potential guerrilla attacks on British bases. These patrols were often compromised, however, by Arab soldiers who realized that the British would soon be gone and their futures would lie in the hands of the guerrillas. The Radfan Mountains were handed over to the Federal Regular Army on June 26, 1967. By November, FLOSY and the NLF were fighting each other. When the Federal Army chose to support the NLF, the future of the country was decided.

Back to Oman

The establishment of a Marxist government in the former Aden Protectorate virtually guaranteed that the Sultan of Oman would once again face an insurgency. A guerrilla war had, in fact, come across the border from what was then the People's Republic of Southern Yemen, later the People's Democratic Republic of Yemen, in 1965 to the Dhofar Mountains of Oman and by 1969 was a serious threat to Oman's security. Additionally, Iraqis had arrived on the Musandam Peninsula and were attempting to raise and train guerrillas. The SAS was committed via HALO and Small Boat Troops to eliminate the Iraqi threat to the Musandam Peninsula, which was located in a position to allow interdiction of the Persian Gulf from its shores. Although the Iraqi threat was eliminated rather easily, that from the Dhofari guerrillas proved much more serious.

The old Sultan's attempt to keep the country ignorant and backward had given the agitators in South Yemen substantial ammunition for forming a guerrilla movement. In Dhofar, there were no medical facilities and no schools. The population lived in extreme poverty, and anyone who did leave to receive an education could not return. Not only did the tough hill tribesmen make willing insurgents, but they made excellent guerrilla fighters. Rather than attempt to win the guerrillas through any type of reform, the Sultan instead preferred draconian collective punishments, such as cementing over the wells of villages supporting the guerrillas, an especially harsh measure in arid Oman. Villages were also burned and guerrilla corpses were hung in the city of Salalah along the

Member of the World War II SBS offers a good view of the beret as worn at that time. IWM

coastal plain. An assassination attempt against the Sultan by his own bodyguards, along with the audacity the guerrillas were showing in laying mines and carrying out ambushes, finally led Qaboos, with British support, to overthrow his father in July 1967 and begin much-needed reforms.

Even before the change of ruler in Oman, a small group of SAS officers had started planning for operations in Oman. Their plan was a classic counterinsurgency one, combining military with civil action. Broken into five primary components, the plan called for medical assistance to the Dhofaris, veterinary assistance for their livestock, increased sources of water, an intelligence-gathering campaign, and psychological operations to remove support for the guerrillas, combined with an amnesty campaign to allow disenchanted guerrillas to turn themselves in.

Almost as soon as the old Sultan was deposed, a small SAS team was sent to Salalah, where in addition to laying the foundation for a counterinsurgency campaign, they also acted as Qaboos's bodyguards for awhile. One of their first counterinsurgency moves was to drop leaflets offering amnesty, a tactic that quickly bore fruit when one of the most effective guerrillas surrendered, bringing invaluable intelligence. As the campaign progressed, the SAS team arranged to have cheap transistor radios sold to the Dhofaris—so that they could hear truthful newscasts about the reforms being undertaken under Qaboos and the various civic action programs being implemented. These broadcasts undercut propaganda broadcasts from across the border with South Yemen.

At this point, SAS personnel were there on training rather than combat patrols. Their primary contributions were medical assistance on the plains below the mountains and other civil actions. The first SAS troops also established a model farm at Salalah, where they brought in two bulls to help increase the size of Dhofari cattle. These experiences proved the importance of fluent communications, and members of squad-rons sent in later underwent ten weeks of training in Arabic.

As more tribesmen accepted amnesty—in many cases because the Communist guerrillas tried to make them give up Islam—the SAS began training and forming "firqats" of turned guerrillas to operate against their former comrades. Between September 1970 and March 1971, more than 200 came over.

The firqats became targets of guerrilla operations, particularly at the town of Mirbat where a massive guerrilla assault was launched on July 18, 1972, against the ten-man British Army training team there, scheduled to leave for the United Kingdom the next day. Carrying out civil action as well as training and advising the local firqat, this team shared Mirbat with a detachment of thirty of the Sultan's troops and twenty-five Gendarmerie, as well as the local firqat.

During the night of July 18, this mixed force was hit by 250 guerrillas armed with machine guns, mortars, recoilless rifles, and rocket launchers. They infiltrated before attacking so that they could hit the defenses from all sides. Their first target were eight Gendarmerie on guard duty above the town. Although four of this group were killed in the initial attack, they managed to get off shots to warn the garrison at Mirbat. Having lost their surprise, the guerrillas proceeded to mortar Mirbat. Awakened, the SAS team began firing upon the attackers. Captain Mike Kealy, commanding the team, realized this was a major assault and radioed for assistance. Meanwhile, two Fijian members of the SAS were helping bring the lone 25lb gun near the Gendarmerie fort into action. As 84mm Carl Gustav rounds from guerrilla rocket launchers hit one of the two forts on the outskirts of Mirbat, other guerrillas were breaking through the perimeter wire around the town. The Gendarmerie fort continued to hold, however.

When he noticed that the large gun had grown silent, Kealy and a team medic went to check on the situation, finding both SAS men and an Omani artilleryman wounded. Corporal Labalaba, one of the Fijians, was still attempting to keep the gun in action, but he was soon killed. The medical orderly subsequently took a severe hit that shot away his jaw, leaving Kealy and Trooper Ti to defend the emplacement alone. Just as they were about to be overrun, air support arrived. Kealy quickly placed air identification panels and guided in air strikes and called in mortar fire from a member of the SAS team. As the jets strafed the guerrilla firing positions above Mirbat, SAS reinforcements arrived. These reinforcements were drawn from G Squadron, which had just arrived at Salalah and had been preparing to check their weapons for functioning and accuracy. By the time the area had been secured, two of the SAS defenders had been killed and two were wounded. The battle would pass into SAS legend. Six Omanis had also been killed, along with four members of a firqat patrol that had encountered the retreating guerrillas on their way back to Mirbat. At least half of the guerrilla attacking force, which had been drawn from the best fighters the guerrillas could muster, were casualties, thus inflicting a severe morale blow to the insurgents.

The firqats began establishing their bases in some of the best locations on the plateau. Well-supplied with water and having a clinic and a shop to sell food and other items, these encampments soon proved magnets for the civilian population. The civilians found them so beneficial, too, that the guerrillas would have risked losing their base of support had they attacked them. As the firqats and the Sultan's armed forces gained control of Dhofar, the guerrillas were driven toward the South Yemen border. The civic action campaign, now involving mobile well-drilling teams and agricultural advisors, helped make sure the areas remained secure.

As they became more successful, however, the firqats attempted to become more conventional, demanding air and artillery support and thus losing much of their advantage of speed and stealth. Still, the firqats and the SAS played a key role in the last major battle for control of a cave complex used by the guerrillas as a storage depot. Although fighting around this complex lasted for weeks, it was eventually denied the guerrillas.

Although the SAS was denied any cross-border operations into Yemen, one ex-SAS officer on contract to the Sultan established a string of agents who operated in South Yemen and throughout Dhofar. Among the operations carried out by his irregulars was the blowing up of a fort eighty miles inside South Yemen. Meanwhile, the area of guerrilla operations continued to shrink until in October 1975, the final operations to clear areas near the South Yemen border were launched, cutting guerrilla supply lines and effectively ending the insurgency. After the SAS left Oman in September 1976, many of the functions it had carried out were absorbed by former SAS men on contract to the Sultan.

The SAS had proven quite effective in the dual role of medical and agricultural advisers and practitioners at the most basic level and as organizers and leaders of the irregular firqats. With the maximum number of SAS soldiers in

the country at one time normally between seventy and eighty, the regiment had exerted an influence on the outcome of the counterinsurgency campaign far out of proportion to its numbers. Oman had also re-established the traditional SAS association with the desert and shown along with the Borneo campaign that the regiment could carry out sensitive counterinsurgency missions in support of British allies.

The Liberation of Kuwait

Ironically, as the invasion of Kuwait was launched, a small detachment of about ten SAS soldiers was on its way there to carry out an advisory and training mission. Reportedly, their flight landed in Kuwait City a few hours after the invasion had begun, allowing them to fade into the desert. Some reports allege that they carried out intelligence operations, while others state that they escaped and proceeded to Saudi Arabia. As trained SAS soldiers, it's quite likely that finding themselves in the midst of the invasion, they did a little of both. During the campaign in Kuwait and Iraq, the SAS would carry out many of its traditional desert missions, including establishing observation posts and gathering intelligence on Iraqi units, as well as deploying laser designators for various targets, including SCUD launchers. Using their language skills and experience of the Middle East, members of the SAS also disguised themselves as Arabs and infiltrated urban areas to assess everything from enemy morale to bomb damage. During these operations, four SAS men were killed and three others were captured and tortured.

The first large contingent of British special forces personnel arrived in August 1990, when a C-130 flew in detachments of the SAS and the Special Boat Squadron. Both units immediately began operating in the desert. Had the Iraqis invaded Saudi Arabia, the SAS and US Special Forces would have carried out raids on their lo-

Members of the SBS check their weapons before an operation in the Aegean. IWM

gistical and communications systems. Another SAS mission was to find out what types of chemical weapons the Iraqis had in their inventory so that antidotes could be found and be ready for use. As the special operations mission expanded, by December 1990, the SAS A, B, and D Squadrons were deployed to the desert, leaving just G Squadron on alert for the counterterrorist mission. Some Territorial Army SAS personnel were also deployed, as well as specialist SAS Signals Troops, totaling about 400 in all.

Most SAS missions were launched out of the Saudi air base at Al Jubail, including raids into western Iraq and operations against SCUD launchers. Part of the SAS mission was to strike behind the enemy lines and tie down resources on security duties. The mobility granted by their Land Rovers and Light Strike Vehicles enabled them to carry out hit-and-run raids with their usual efficiency against Iraqi communication sites, convoys, and supply dumps. Air strikes were called in against SCUDs, and communication cables between Baghdad and western Iraq were blown up, thus forcing the Iraqis to use radio communication that could be jammed or intercepted. The SAS and the US Delta Force, it should be noted, found a substantial number of the SCUDs that were destroyed.

Meanwhile, the SBS was operating with its US counterparts, the Navy SEALs, to convince the Iraqis that the US Marines were going to invade Kuwait from the sea. The SBS would also have the honor of recapturing the British embassy in Kuwait City.

The war against Iraq allowed the SAS to test its current desert equipment in a combat environment and use many of the tactics to guide in "smart" ordnance developed originally for NATO. The SAS and SBS also got to work in conjunction with their US counterparts in combat to test the joint tactics they had practiced for many years. Most importantly, the SAS proved once again that it could still operate very effectively in the desert against the enemy's communications and transport.

Chapter 4

Jungle Warriors

Malaya

A 1946 study of future roles for the British Army determined the need for a unit capable of operating behind enemy lines, as the SAS had done in World War II. Interestingly, this study specifically stated that, contrary to popular opinion, the SAS would not drain off potential leaders from other units but would take many of the soldiers who did not function well in traditional regiments. Because the Army was cutting units, however, the SAS's continued existence was as a reserve or Territorial Army (TA) regiment rather than as a regular one. As a result, in 1947, the 21st SAS (Artists) was formed. The members of this unit were traditionally drawn from London's painters, sculptors, writers, and others affiliated with the creative arts. The 21st SAS has always been known for its individualistic, intelligent, creative soldiers, and some Artists traditions continue with 21st SAS to this day, including mounting guard for the opening of the annual Royal Academy's Summer Exhibition. The "21" came from the two wartime regiments: no. 1 and no. 2. Even though the wartime regiments had ceased to exist, it should be noted that 2nd SAS's Intelligence Section was still carrying out its mission of tracking down Nazi war criminals, particularly those who had implemented the Commando Order. The 21st SAS drew quite well from experienced SAS soldiers, 180 wartime veterans joining its ranks, including many officers who joined as enlisted personnel. It was assumed that in wartime, the SAS would expand to corps strength with its TA cadre as the basis.

The counterinsurgency war in Malaya represented the resurrection of the SAS as a regular regiment in the British Army. Initially, the first SAS contingent to arrive in Malaya—M Squadron—had not even been intended for that campaign but was on its way to Korea. Even though the SAS had no experience in jungle warfare, its reputation as excellent Special Operations Troops had convinced MacArthur to ask for the unit to be assigned to Korea. The Communist Terrorists (CTs) the colonial government in Malaya was facing had been escalating its guerrilla campaign since 1948, and the vital rubber and tin industries as well as the government were now threatened. Between 5,000 and 10,000 guerrillas were now using the jungle, which covered three-quarters of the country, as their base, by 1950 killing 1,200. A unit that could take the war to the enemy was needed, and the SAS seemed to fit the requirement.

Most of the British infantry regiments then serving in Malaya were being used in static defensive roles, a mission with little real effect on combating an insurgency based on Mao's pre-

US Special Forces MACV SOG Reconnaissance Teams such as this one shared their experiences with the SAS, just as SAS teams in Borneo shared theirs with the Special Forces. Reportedly, at least a few members of the British SAS went on missions with SOG as members of the "Australian SAS." Society of Vietnamese Rangers

US Special Forces four-man elements operate much as the SAS four-man patrol, keeping security in all directions while using the stream bed to avoid leaving tracks. US Special Forces members train for small unit operations much as SAS patrols do, the two units exchanging tactics and personnel constantly. US Army

cepts of winning the countryside first. The French, particularly, would be defeated in Indochina due to an excessive reliance on static security. Another problem was that many of the CT leaders had fought as guerrillas against the Japanese, often alongside British troops, and, therefore, were quite familiar with British tactics. Once again in fairly standard guerrilla style, the CTs terrorized the aborigines living in the jungle, forcing them to provide food and to act as an early warning system for British operations.

The usefulness of a unit capable of operating in small patrols deep in the jungle had been illustrated by the locally formed "Ferret Force," which included some SOE jungle fighting veterans among its ranks. Many members of Ferret

Force, however, rotated to other duties. Major Mike Calvert, who had been an SAS brigadier during the war, had been assigned to study the guerrilla war in Malaya and offer suggestions for the best method to defeat the CTs. Among his suggestions were that a protected village plan be implemented to deny the CTs village support and also protect the villagers from the guerrillas. This would be the basis for what would come to be known as the "Briggs Plan," named after the general under whose command it was implemented. Eventually, most villagers living on the outskirts of the jungle were moved to new villages farther away, thus denying the CTs a vital source of food, manpower, and intelligence. Such forced movement has backfired in some cases, but in Malaya, the new villages were designed to improve the lifestyles of the villagers and, thus, received wide acceptance.

Calvert also saw the advantages of forming a deep penetration unit to harry the CTs in the jungle. The result was the Malayan Scouts, which included SOE and SAS veterans, as well as former French Foreign Legionaries among its early recruits. Additionally, Calvert recruited 120 volunteers from Rhodesia who would form C Squadron. Many who would assume positions of importance during Rhodesia's counterinsurgency war gained their first experience as members of C Squadron. New Zealanders, including many Maoris, would later replace the Rhodesians when they returned to their own country. To support the Malayan Scouts, Calvert also formed an intelligence section incorporating many old Asia hands.

Such was the situation when the first SAS Squadron arrived in Singapore to join with the Malayan Scouts. Agreeing with J. M. Woodhouse, Calvert had concluded that two essential elements were necessary to defeat the CTs. First, the aborigines—the Sakai, as they were derogatorily known in Malay—would have to be won over and moved to safe areas, and, second, the CT's combat potential had to be destroyed by ambushing them as they left the jungle and relentlessly pursuing them to their bases. This required exceptional stalking skills; hence, Calvert and Woodhouse developed a realistic training regimen. One of their most effective methods was to arm two troopers with air rifles, and then send them into a prearranged area of the jungle to stalk each other. Although they wore fencing masks to protect their eyes and faces, substantial skin was left exposed to feel the sting of mistakes. This technique is still practiced, although wax bullets have been substituted in the last few years. Not only do such exercises inculcate stalking skills, but they also help duplicate the adrenaline flow of stalking an enemy in a kill-or-be-killed environment, teaching the subject controlled breathing, sound discipline, and other lessons. Calvert, himself, however, did not get to see the success of the measures he had put into effect; contracting various tropical diseases, he was sent home.

Before the SAS began sending deep penetration patrols into the Malayan jungle, conventional wisdom was that European troops could operate in that environment for only three weeks at a time. SAS patrols would evolve to the point where they could remain in the jungle virtually indefinitely, sometimes tracking the enemy for months on end. Carrying minimal supplies and ammunition, they could rely on their bush survival training to live off the land. On deep penetration patrols, resupply was normally accomplished via airdrops, if at all. Also developed for SAS jungle patrols was the seven- to fourteen-day ration, a forerunner of the British Battle Ration.

The SAS also developed a hearts-and-minds campaign to win the jungle-dwelling aborigines

One of the most effective SAS training techniques in Malaya was fitting troops out with fencing masks and air rifles and letting them stalk each other. IWM

*Sergeant Turnbull, the famed SAS tracker in Malaya,
with his kit and the Browning shotgun he wielded so
effectively.* IWM

to their side and deny their assistance to the CTs. As the US Special Forces would find later in Vietnam, the SAS found that offering medical assistance and helping the tribesmen defend themselves from the guerrillas, along with attempting to learn their language and customs, were the two primary requirements for gaining their trust. The fact that many of the CTs were Chinese also helped isolate them from much of the population who were Malay or aboriginal. The aborigines became active sources of intelligence about CT movements. Although some local tribesmen acted as trackers, this assistance was mostly provided by Ibans from Borneo. Many SAS troopers also became expert jungle trackers, particularly Sergeant Turnbull, who was known for his ability to follow a track for weeks until finally getting the kill. Turnbull was also one of many SAS troops in Malaya who made effective use of the twelve-gauge shotgun for ambushes and counterambushes in the jungle. Reportedly, special loads incorporating buckshot surrounded by smaller shot were used to increase CT casualty rates. Often in counterinsurgency warfare, where the guerrillas normally do not have an effective medical service, severe wounds are more detrimental than kills since injured guerrillas are a drain on those still attempting to fight and are also demoralizing. The SAS became proficient, too, at turning a traditional guerrilla tactic—planting booby traps—against the CTs. SAS soldiers booby trapped CT fish traps with explosives, and once even booby trapped a turtle caught in one of the traps to blow up when the CTs prepared it to eat!

To get at the CTs deep in the jungle, SAS patrols often had to walk long distances. They also used jungle waterways and were occasionally inserted by helicopters, although these were retained primarily for medical evacuation and resupply. The jungle canopy in Malaya made the traditional method of inserting SAS patrols by parachute dangerous. Nevertheless, often small clearings under cultivation in the jungle indicated that guerrillas were camped nearby. To confirm this intelligence, a patrol immediately had to be inserted in the exact area.

Since much of Malaya is covered with trees rising to 200ft, with interlocking branches, the SAS felt it imperative to develop a new parachute jumping technique. Thus was born "treejumping," in which SAS troops deliberately would parachute into the trees and then lower themselves to the ground. The first SAS operational jump in Malaya was in February 1952. That was the same year that the Malayan Scouts were officially designated the 22nd SAS Regiment. It should be noted, however, that some of the original Malayan Scouts proved unsatisfactory as SAS troops, thus reinforcing the SAS view that each member of the regiment should pass rigorous selection.

The earliest jumps were made with a 100ft rope as the only special equipment. SAS paratroopers Hugh Mercer, John Cooper, and Alastair MacGregor were among those conducting experiments to develop the most effective and safe means of carrying out such jumps. The result was the evolution of a special tree-jumping harness made for the SAS in a Singapore prison. To practice descent techniques, a Bailey Bridge was upended in Kuala Lumpur. The issue version of this special abseiling kit took 40min to prepare before a jump. Consisting of canvas "bikini" shorts which the jumper put on and adjusted by straps and a 240ft roll of webbed tape, with a tensile strength of 1000lb, the rig was quite ingenious. The tape was carried in the weapons container and passed through a steel ring in the front of the bikini. Once through the ring, it was threaded first through a canvas "tunnel" around the soldier's waist and then through the ring again. About 6ft of tape was pulled through and secured to the parachute harness. After jumping and being caught in a tree, the SAS trooper secured the 6ft length of tape to a strong branch and threw the rest to the ground. Next, the weapon container was lowered to the ground, a practice that left the jumper somewhat vulnerable at this point and caused some treejumpers to carry a pistol as well as a rifle, shotgun, or submachine gun. Once rid of the weapon container, the jumper could then release himself from his parachute harness and remain dangling from the tape,

Tree jumper preparing his harness before a jump in Malaya. Special Air Service

which he then paid out through the steel ring to lower himself to the ground. The rate of descent was controlled by the friction of the tape passing through the ring and the canvas tunnel. Light pressure with one hand on the tape would normally arrest the descent if necessary.

Once on the ground, the jumper destroyed or buried his tree-jumping rig so that the CTs could not make use of it, and then started his patrol. As a result, a new kit had to be prepared for each jump. Some improvements were made in the kit as it evolved, including one design incorporating rollers on the chest so that the parachutist could safely be lowered to the ground even if he passed out from injuries after securing his tape.

The SAS has rarely had to resort to tree-jumps since Malaya, although the technique they pioneered is now a standard part of most special force soldiers' parachuting repertoire.

By 1958, after operating in Malaya for eight years, the SAS had grown accustomed to the heavy rainfall, tropical temperatures, and resultant humidity. They could operate well in the jungle or in the swamps, where they learned to construct "bashas" in the roots of large trees growing above the water. These offered not only a dry place in which to sleep, but also protection from sneak attack, as movement through the surrounding water would be detected. As of 1958, the CTs had been forced onto the defensive, with 9,000 already killed or captured and only 2,000 remaining at large and driven deep into the swamps. In fact, many of the most dangerous remaining CTs were in encampments deep in the Telok Anson Swamp. As a result, 1958 saw an SAS squadron with Iban trackers and such SAS members as the indefatigable Sergeant Turnbull, who followed one spoor for fourteen weeks, penetrate to this and other remote areas to burn the CT hideouts and kill or capture most of the leaders. One troop leader during these operations was Captain Peter de la Billiere, who would later serve as the brigadier general commanding all three SAS regiments.

The insurgency now virtually defeated except for a few holdouts along the Thai border, virtually all of the SAS troops remaining in Malaya were rotated back to Great Britain. The maximum SAS commitment had been five squadrons, each with 112 troops, yet they had exerted an influence on the campaign out of proportion to their numbers. The SAS's ability to operate in the jungle set an example for other Commonwealth troops to extend their own operations. The SAS also performed two invaluable counterinsurgency functions in that their hearts-and-minds campaign helped deny the CTs local support and their deep penetration patrols denied the guerrillas a safe haven. SAS patrols often acted as the "beaters" to drive CTs into ambushes set by the Gurkhas or other British units. Many precepts developed by the SAS in Malaya became standard for the SAS in later counterinsurgency campaigns, as well as for the United States in Vietnam and Latin America. Perhaps most importantly, the success of the SAS in Malaya established the continued need for such special operations units.

Borneo

When it began to appear that Borneo might be the site of the next jungle war calling for the SAS's special skills, J. M. Woodhouse, who had helped preside over the resurgence of the SAS in Malaya, was commanding 22nd SAS. With Indonesian President Sukarno and his powerful armed forces threatening British protectorates in Northern Borneo, including Sarawak, Sabah, and Brunei, it was becoming apparent by late 1962 that British assistance would be needed to thwart his plan to include Malaysia, the new federated state consisting of Malaya, Singapore, Sarawak, and Sabah, in his "Greater Indonesia." The Chinese Communists, who had provided the hard core for the insurgency in Malaya, also proved the most fertile recruiting ground for Sukarno's agents in Northern Borneo. In addition to agents, the Indonesians infiltrated saboteurs across the border.

Those recruited as potential guerrillas were then taken just across the border into the Indonesian portion of Borneo, known as Kalimantan, to receive training in small groups. Once trained, they were formed into cells of the Clandestine Communist Organization (CCO). Also recruited to assist the CCO and the Indonesians were the remnants of TNKU, a guerrilla movement that had unsuccessfully attempted to wrest control of Brunei from the Sultan in 1962.

The SAS was chosen for service in Borneo for several reasons, the most compelling of which were probably the regiment's successful counterinsurgency experience in the jungle during the Malayan campaign and their possession of new long-range radios allowing them to communicate with the United Kingdom while operating in Borneo. The SAS's ability to work with indigenous populations, no doubt was also a factor. In any case, Woodhouse offered A Squadron to Major General Walter Walker, the astute director of operations, who accepted, although his initial plan would have misused the SAS as a mobile parachute reserve had Woodhouse not persuaded him that his troops would be much better used as the basis for small, early warning patrols along the border with Indonesian Borneo. The border was so long, in fact, that it would require small SAS observation posts as well as a successful hearts-and-minds campaign to gain the assistance of local villagers to multiple the eyes and ears deployed along the border. After its arrival in January 1963, A Squadron's commanding officer soon walked hundreds of kilometers of the border alone to determine the most effective use of his limited, although highly skilled, resources. Although Walker may not have initially understood the SAS's capabilities, he soon became a convert and eventually stated his belief that during the "confrontation," as the near-war with Indonesia was euphemistically called, each SAS troop was equal in value to a battalion of infantry.

In gaining the support of local villagers, the SAS worked with Tom Harrison, who during World War II had led local guerrillas against the Japanese and then later against TNKU. Veteran SAS members also renewed contacts with some of the former Sarawak Rangers they had known in Malaya. So efficient did their lo-

SAS men go out the door on a jump in Malaya. IWM

Members of the Rhodesian SAS use a bamboo raft to move along a river in Malaya. Rhodesian SAS Association

cal network become that the SAS squadron was covering 700 miles of border with their aid. Among the techniques used by the SAS to gain local support were their traditional use of the local language—in this case Malay, which many spoke—medical assistance, and respect for local customs. The SAS found especially that in Borneo, gaining the trust of the village leader by showing him proper deference was important. Two or four SAS men lived near each local village providing border watchers, and their daily contact built trust. In some cases, along the border the SAS operated in groups of six, divided into a couple of two-man surveillance teams and a two-man communications team. The surveillance teams had the task of spotting infiltrators and following them to fix their position so that heavier forces could eliminate them. Should heavier infantry be needed to counter an incursion, the Gurkhas provided heliborne reaction forces.

On August 12, 1963, thirty guerrillas infiltrated and attacked a police station and looted the bazaar at Tebedu in West Sarawak. Although led by Indonesians, the raiders left pamphlets claiming to have been members of TNKU. The number of successes such as this would be few, however, as the SAS intelligence network expanded. Border scouts were formed to help gather intelligence, and Dyak traders who passed back and forth across the border with Indonesia were also recruited. Nevertheless, 700 miles was too much for a single squadron. As a result, two of the SAS squadrons that had been cut at the end of the Malayan Emergency were re-established. B Squadron was recruited from among British Army of the Rhine soldiers, while the Guards Independent Parachute Company formed the basis for what would become G Squadron.

Additionally, SAS personnel became available for Sarawak and Sabah when they joined the Malayan Federation since it was a part of SEATO. As a result, New Zealand and Australia each sent SAS troops to Borneo. The New Zea-land Maoris proved especially adept as trackers. With the New Zealand and Australian SAS troops helping in Sarawak and Sabah, members of D Squadron were spread a little less thinly and could now also begin raising and training local tribal militia.

Occasional incursions still were successful. In December 1963, for example, 125 guerrillas, including members of the Indonesian Marines, attacked a Royal Malay Regiment outpost in Sabah, although they were eventually wiped out by the 1/10 Gurkha Rifles. The fact that Indonesian regulars had been involved did cause the SAS to move back into the mountains of central Sarawak. Then, in early 1964, the SAS was given approval to begin cross-border reconnaissance operations to find the camps from which guerrilla incursions were being launched. To keep their activities clandestine, however, it was understood that should any of the SAS members be captured they would claim they had wandered across the border by misreading their map. Should they get into a firefight with the Indonesians, they were to rapidly break contact and retreat back across the border. So successful were these reconnaissance missions that the SAS was sent across the border to find the river routes the Indonesians used to transport men and equipment to the border. The SAS tried to sterilize their area of operations, leaving no trace of their presence. So that neither the sound nor spent cartridge cases of their rifles could give them away, they were equipped with the same Armalite rifles (basically the US M-16) the Indonesians were using. To camouflage their footprints, they either altered the tread on their boots to match that of Indonesian combat boots or covered the soles with sacking. To this day, the US Special Forces and SAS, long-time allies and friends, speculate about the possibility of US and SAS soldiers firing at each other on these incursions, as some US Special Forces soldiers were advising the Indonesian Special Forces at this time. To increase cross-border in-

Members of the Rhodesian SAS loading their equipment on a plane in Malaya. Note the monkey, which was their mascot. Rhodesian SAS Association

On jungle operations, members of the SAS are trained to remain ever vigilant. Here, one man stands guard, while the other cleans their mess tins. Special Air Service

telligence-gathering capability, the SAS also trained forty Ibans in late summer 1964 to operate across the Indonesian border.

Some cross-border operations lasted up to three weeks and were so debilitating that even tough, experienced SAS soldiers could normally handle only three of them before rotating back to the United Kingdom. Generally, there was about a week's recovery time between the patrols.

To punish the Indonesians even more, in June 1964, "claret" operations, which would include ambushes and booby traps on the Indonesian side of the border, were authorized. These operations were classified top secret and were done under strict guidelines. Initially, they could penetrate only 3,000m, a distance later

upped to 6km and eventually to 10km. The primary mission of those on claret operations was to harass and intimidate the Indonesians into moving their camps back from the border, thus making incursions more easy to detect and stop. Usually, claret patrols were led by members of the SAS, with the bulk of the "teeth" comprised of Gurkhas. Additionally, the SAS set ambushes and booby traps along trails inside Indonesian territory, tapped phone lines to gather intelligence, and snatched prisoners.

Claret operations were successful enough that they helped destabilize Sukarno, who was removed by an Army coup in March 1966. At this point, the SAS, in conjunction with MI6, was already planning a series of guerrilla operations on Sumatra and Java that would have tied down even more Indonesian troops. By August 1966, peace had been declared. During the "confrontation," total Commonwealth deaths had amounted to 114, seven of them SAS, including one reportedly captured and murdered. Indonesian and guerrilla deaths numbered about 2,000.

In carrying out its highly successful counterinsurgency/counterinfiltration campaign in Borneo, the SAS had certain very real advantages. Thanks to the recent success in Malaya, the Regiment knew how to fight a jungle counterguerrilla campaign. The SAS even provided scouts for the Gurkhas, who proved to be quite good in the jungle themselves. Additionally, the SAS was quite skillful at gaining the trust of local populations and winning their support and active assistance. Once again, too, the SAS proved its ability to be deployed to an environment considered very hostile by most troops and then rapidly to turn that environment to its advantage.

Other Jungles, Other Times

The SAS has continued to emphasize its jungle capabilities. An important part of SAS selection and training takes place in the jungles of Brunei, and SAS members have attended jungle survival and training courses around the world. Deployments to jungle environments have continued, although sometimes with little

During jungle operations, members of the Special Air Service received a briefing. Special Air Service

publicity. SAS troops, for example, have been sent to Belize for "training" in the jungle, especially when Honduras asserts its claims to this former British possession. At least a few members of the SAS saw service in Vietnam as well, although they were usually either uniformed as Australian or New Zealand SAS or US Special Forces. Although the Rhodesian War was not really a jungle war, it had aspects of jungle warfare, and members of the Rhodesian SAS and Selous Scouts who either had previously served with 21st, 22nd, or 23d SAS participated. At least some veterans of this war later served in 22nd SAS as well.

Chapter 5

Europe and the South Atlantic

World War II in Europe

The image of the SAS in the desert has become so ingrained that the exploits of the SAS during the liberation of Europe have often been relegated to semi-obscurity. This may be explained at least partially by the fact that so many other special units were operating behind the German lines. There was a distinct difference, however, between most of the clandestine operatives parachuted into occupied Europe and the SAS patrols operating there. The SAS, particularly, remained a uniformed military formation, even though it operated for extended periods some distance behind enemy lines. At times, too, the SAS cooperated with the various clandestine groups, helping them train resistance fighters and carrying out reconnaissance and raids. Throughout, the SAS remained a military unit much more responsive to strategic objectives and more amenable to control—a somewhat ironic distinction, since the SAS had developed quite a reputation for its individualism.

SAS operations in Greece and, to a lesser extent, Italy have been mentioned previously, but it was in France that SAS patrols were used most frequently and most effectively during the later stages of the war. Other northern European countries would see limited SAS commitment. As "Operation Overlord" neared, the

During operations in Europe and Italy, SAS Jeep Patrols could be inserted via parachute or glider, and then could harass the German logistical and communications network. IWM

availability of parachute-qualified SAS units offered SHAEF the option of inserting them to gather intelligence or to strike at strategic targets. Nevertheless, for logistical purposes, just as they had been assigned to the Long-Range Desert Group in North Africa, the SAS was assigned to the British First Airborne Division prior to D-Day. The SAS did not, however, jump nor did they fight as part of the First Airborne. Instead, SAS troops were normally dropped in small parties behind German lines, and once they completed these missions, tried to make their way back to Allied lines, stayed in place and waited for the advancing Allied armies to reach them, or received aerial resupply and continued to conduct additional missions.

Cooperating first with French and then with Dutch resistance groups, SAS soldiers established bases in forests near good parachute drop zones. From these bases, SAS patrols could operate over hundreds of square miles to raid and disrupt German communications and supply. The largest SAS bases were established in Brittany, the Forest of Orleans, the Grand Massif, the Forest of Chatillon, outside of Poitiers, and near Vosges. From D-Day until the German surrender, SAS patrols saw action in France, Italy, Belgium, Holland, and Germany, accounting for 7,733 enemy dead or seriously wounded, 4,784 prisoners, 700 motor vehicles destroyed or captured, seven trains destroyed and thirty-three derailed, and 164 raillines cut. Additionally, the SAS helped capture 18,000 Germans at Issoudun, when they helped block all escape routes. SAS information allowed the RAF to bomb eleven fuel trains, twelve ammunition dumps, a flying bomb site, two enemy air bases, an SS Barracks (resulting in 300 SS killed), and a radio station. Twice, too, SAS patrols located their old enemy from the desert, Field Marshal Erwin Rommel, pinpointing his headquarters for bomb attacks, which disrupted the coordination of the German defense of France.

The first plan involving deployment of the SAS had been to drop a few dozen men along with hundreds of dummies on Pas De Calais in conjunction with the Normandy landings to help reinforce the German preconception that the primary invasion would take place there. Late in the planning process, however, it was decided to use only the dummies and save the SAS for other tasks.

The first of these tasks fell to the SAS on June 6, 1944, when 144 SAS soldiers were parachuted, along with Jeeps and supplies, into an area near Dijon in an operation code-named "Houndsmith." These patrols blew up numerous railway lines to hamper transport of reinforcements and supplies to the front, taking more than 100 German prisoners and killing or wounding 220 more. Additionally, the SAS "guerrillas" spotted juicy targets for the RAF. Also launched on June 6 was "Bulbasket," involving fifty members of the SAS near Chateauroux.

Later operations included "Cooney" on June 7, in which eighteen three- to six-man parties were dropped between St. Malo and Vannes to harass communications and blow up key installations. A week later on June 14, "Garn" inserted fifty-eight men, who drove through the German rear areas between Raµbouillet and Chartres, attacking truck convoys and blowing up raillines. The largest of the SAS missions did not occur until late in the war when "Amherst" began on April 6, 1945. The Germans were then retreating through Holland, and the SAS was to prevent them from forming a coherent defense and to protect key bridges and airfields so that the retreating Germans did not destroy them. Although 700 men were dropped at nineteen different locations, "Amherst" lasted for only 72

hours. Nevertheless, in subsequent fighting, the SAS accounted for German casualties almost equal to their own numbers, while suffering only ninety-three casualties in the process.

Although there were other larger and more successful operations (when measured in the number of enemy dead) encompassing more men, perhaps the best SAS operation in northern Europe for illustrating how the Jeep Patrols were used was "Wallace." This operation, which would eventually prove to be the deepest SAS Jeep penetration in France, started with the American breakthrough at Avranches. Twenty SAS Jeeps equipped with oversized gas tanks, granting a range of up to 900 miles and each mounting five Vickers machine guns were airlifted with their three-man crews to Rennes Airfield. The commander of "Wallace" was Ray Farran, whose book *Winged Dagger* is one of the best about the SAS during World War II and whose experiences in Palestine after the war helped lay the groundwork for SAS undercover operations.

Staying on country lanes, well away from main thoroughfares, the column passed through occupied territory on its way to the SAS base in the forests near Chatillon. Unfortunately, they soon encountered a German Panzer Division and, although they fought well, lost thirteen Jeeps. When they finally reached their base, they joined with a small group of SAS men who had been operating from it for more than a month. Now having a combined strength of ten Jeeps and sixty men, this raiding party ventured forth daily to mine roads, knock out trucks, and attack German radar installations. Another favorite tactic was to quietly approach a German headquarters at night and give the Nazis a wake-up call with their 3in mortars.

As the SAS party established local contacts, they began operating with the Maquis to ambush larger German supply convoys. Eight more Jeeps had been dropped to reinforce Farran's party; hence, an attack was launched on the town of Chatillon, killing more than 100 Germans. The SAS made it a point to have a substantial number of their Maquis allies present during the drop so that the French would believe the Jeeps had come by air, rather than assuming that the SAS were scouts for an advancing Allied division.

After hitting Chatillon, the "Wallace" group moved on toward the Belfort Gap, where the Germans were retreating from the 3rd and 7th Armies. Along their route, the SAS Jeep Patrols continued to destroy fuel dumps or any other target of opportunity that they encountered. When their Jeeps broke down from hard usage, French mechanics working in German motorpools would be summoned by the Resistance. Bringing stolen German spare parts, the mechanics would improvise to make the needed repairs. Finally, after more than a month behind German lines, they linked up with the 7th Army, which they supplied with much useful intelligence.

During "Wallace" and more than forty other SAS operations, air drops of supplies were an absolute prerequisite for success. The RAF consistently carried out their resupply missions with great dedication, bringing in everything from boots in specified sizes to Jeeps to 6lb antitank guns. Many weapons were already in containers for dropping. A twenty-four-container drop might contain 19,800 rounds of 9mm parabellum and 38,006 rounds of .303 ammunition, 1,116 field dressings (for small groups, more ammunition could be substituted), 240 empty Bren magazines, 124 empty Sten magazines, 145lb of explosives with detonation supplies (time pencils, etc.), four PIAT antitank weapons, 125 PIAT bombs, forty Gammon grenades, eight Bren guns, and ten Sten guns. These drops could, however, be varied to fit special needs in weapons or ammunition. Food, fuel, and daily rum rations were also included. Even though the SAS patrols frequently suffered at the hands of Allied fighter pilots who strafed anything moving on the roads behind the German lines, they realized that the RAF had done a masterful job of keeping them supplied; they found that flying the Union Jack from their antennas and deploying yellow smoke when Allied planes approached helped limit the strafing runs. Some resupply drops did go astray, landing in trees or hedges, but unlike a full-scale airborne assault, when parachutes

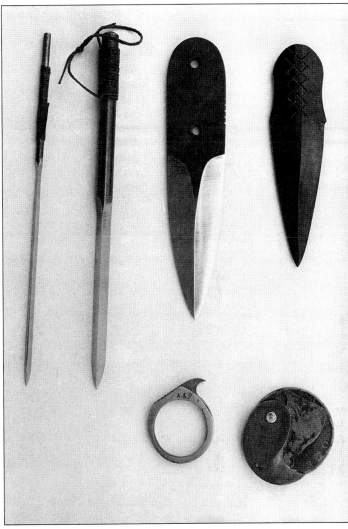

SAS men often carried assorted clandestine knives to help escape and evade. This group from an OSS instructor's kit illustrates many of the basic types. At top left, one that could be hidden inside a pencil; second left, a Commando Nail, often secreted in the fly; third left, a lapel dagger; fourth left, a thumb dagger; at bottom left, a tire slasher; and at bottom right, a slasher secreted on a coin.

may be left lying around, by dawn the SAS had to recover any chutes and erase all evidence of the night drop. Drops were normally arranged

79

by radio, but the SAS also used pigeons to send communications back to Allied units.

It soon began to seem that the SAS were turning up all over occupied France. In Brittany, French members of the SAS raised 40,000 Maquisands, who openly rebelled against the Germans. At one point in central France, ninety SAS men were tying down an entire SS Division searching for them. The operation that endeared the SAS to the French the most, however, occurred when five SAS men in two Jeeps stumbled upon an SS unit in Les Ormes preparing to execute twenty villagers in reprisal for resistance activity. Charging in with their Vickers MGs firing, the SAS rescued eighteen of the villagers, destroying two German trucks and a staff car and killing sixty German soldiers. This small assault was led by D. I. Harrison, another

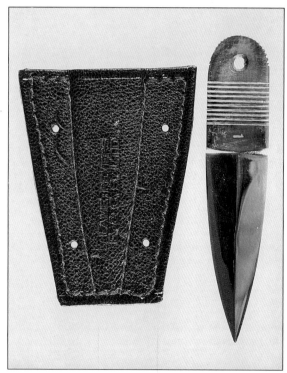

Lapel daggers such as this were often sewn into SAS uniforms for use if captured or as a last-ditch effort during hand-to-hand combat.

chronicler of the SAS in his book *These Men are Dangerous.*

Operations also took place in Italy during the last months of the war. The most impressive was led by Ray Farran, who took a fifty-man party into northwest Italy, where he formed a guerrilla battalion that included escaped POWs, Italian Communists, and others who wanted to kill Germans. This unit harassed the Germans throughout their retreat and supplied Mark Clark's headquarters with useful information. Farran's battalion was even parachuted a 75mm howitzer, which they used to bombard the retreating German columns.

Although operations such as these accounted for extensive German casualties and equipment destroyed, their real value was psychological. The Germans could not feel safe even hundreds of miles behind their own lines, while thousands of troops who should have been deployed against General George Patton, Hodges, or Field Marshall Bernard Montgomery were tied down on garrison duty to prevent SAS raids. Rear area logistical and staff troops also were rendered less effective through constant fear of attacks on their installations. The fear the SAS inspired in the Germans was later put to good use in Norway, where 300,000 Germans remained armed at the end of hostilities. It was feared that fighting would continue, but upon learning that the SAS and other airborne troops were going to be deployed against them, the Germans chose to surrender. The intelligence gathered by SAS patrols and radioed back proved quite valuable as well.

There's also a good chance that word reached Germany that SAS units were moving ahead of Allied forces with the mission of capturing war criminals, thus inspiring many top Nazis to surrender or hastily leave their posts in an attempt to escape. This fear of the SAS also caused the deaths of some SAS soldiers who even though operating in uniform were executed at "terrorists." The worst case happened when thirty members of B Squadron who had been captured at Poitiers were taken into the woods and machine gunned to death. This atrocity was the direct result of Hitler's infa-

SAS raiding parties in occupied Europe often used hit-and-run mortar attacks to good effect. IWM

mous Commando Order, which stated, "these men are very dangerous, and the presence of SAS troops in any area must be immediately reported.... they must be ruthlessly exterminated." As a result of the implementation of the Commando Order, the SAS would designate certain units from their intelligence sections to hunt down Nazis who had carried out such executions. The hunt continued until years after the war—few Nazis being arrested but many being killed! As the SAS was leading the British advance into Germany, this task was often combined with reconnaissance. Allied fears of Hitler's Alpine Redoubt and guerrilla army of "Werewolves" were taken seriously, and SAS patrols knew that counterguerrilla operations against them would be their responsibility if this threat really materialized. Should the Red Army have invaded western Europe, SAS patrols would have been assigned very similar missions, although they might well have had to wear NBC (nuclear, biological, chemical) suits.

Ulster

The SAS was first deployed to Ulster in 1969 with D Squadron. During the few weeks they stayed, the soldiers openly wore their uniforms and ceremoniously placed a wreath on Paddy Mayne's grave. Their primary operations were carried out against Protestant gun smugglers using fishing boats, and they were soon deployed back to the United Kingdom. Over the next two decades, however, the SAS would find itself engaged in a counterinsurgency war in Ulster. The IRA has, in fact, waged a highly successful guerrilla war considering that a relatively small number of truly active members have tied down substantial security forces for so long.

After this first SAS deployment, some members of the Regiment were seconded to intelligence agencies operating in Northern Ireland and to the Military Reconnaissance Force (MRF), which operated in plain clothes. Although the MRF functioned with some success, training was still not up to the standards of the SAS, particularly in close-quarters battle. As a result, in 1974, another squadron of the SAS was deployed to Ulster to reinforce the MRF. The respect and fear the IRA felt for the SAS allowed this Sabre Squadron to exert an influence far larger than its numbers, as the IRA expected SAS ambushes and operations throughout Ulster and, hence, curtailed their operations. In 1976, the SAS was assigned to patrol the border area of South Armagh, known as "Bandit Country" and the area where forty-nine British soldiers had already been killed patrolling. One of the first SAS operations was the establishment of covert observation posts to surveil IRA leaders, arms caches, and IRA rendezvous sites. As is usual with the SAS, sometimes these surveillance teams remained in their hides for weeks at a time.

Within the first year, the SAS operated in South Armagh, four IRA leaders were killed and another six moved across the border into Eire. Even the move across the border didn't always save high-ranking IRA members, however, as the SAS crossed the border to snatch them—although, of course, the IRA denied this, instead claiming that the IRA men "had wandered across the border while intoxicated." SAS patrols also cut security force casualties to a fraction of what they had previously been in the area, although in March 1976, an SAS corporal on surveillance duty was killed because he was a bit slow on the trigger. Many future accusations of an SAS "shoot to kill" policy probably stemmed from this incident, as the SAS were trained, henceforth, to react quickly and violently to any apparent hostile move by the IRA.

By 1977, two SAS squadrons, along with their most high-tech surveillance equipment, were operating in South Armagh and elsewhere in Ulster. Substantial bad publicity resulted after the squadrons were caught on a border crossing and after an Irish teenager was killed.

Consequently, in March 1978, patrols from other regiments were trained to carry out undercover operations in plain clothes so that the SAS presence could be scaled down.

In 1978, a Tasking and Coordination Group had also been set up in Belfast to coordinate the intelligence-gathering operations in Belfast. With better intelligence, SAS ambush teams were now used primarily to catch IRA members in the act of retrieving arms and explosives or of carrying out terrorist acts. During this period, other Army units were also trained to absorb many of the tasks the SAS had been doing. As a result, throughout most of the 1980s, approximately twenty members were deployed to Ulster at any given time. Known as "Ulster Troop," this group carried out the most sensitive ambushes or raids. If a major operation was needed, more SAS men could rapidly be flown in from the United Kingdom. On May 2, 1980, during a house search in Belfast, an SAS officer was killed with a burst from an M-60 MG stolen from a US National Guard armory, but between 1976 and 1987, at least twenty-five IRA members met their deaths at the hands of the SAS.

One of the most impressive of all SAS operations in Ulster was in 1987. In the early part of the year, the IRA had killed numerous Royal Ulster Constabulary (RUC), as well as a high-ranking judge and his wife. As a result, the IRA's credibility was high. Then, British Intelligence learned that two IRA Active Service Units planned to attack a rural RUC station. The theft of a mechanical digger indicated that an attack was imminent and would be like an earlier one in which a digger had been rammed into a police stations before detonating a large explosive device. The most likely targets were identified, and the SAS was deployed in ambush positions near those RUC stations.

Possible targets were narrowed when an RUC surveillance team spotted the digger near the village of Loughgall and witnessed the arrival of 300lb of improvised explosives. As a result, an SAS ambush was set up around the Loughgall RUC station. One SAS team was inside the station with an RUC duty constable, while another team was in a wooded area across

Members of the SAS emplaning before a tree jump in Malaya. IWM

the road. Still other "stop" groups were placed east and west of the station. On May 8, a stolen Toyota van approached the station, running interference for the digger, the bucket of which was now packed with explosives. As the van drew near the station, six IRA men jumped from it and opened fire, while the digger swerved toward the station to plant the explosives. The SAS teams immediately fired upon the terrorists; unfortunately, one civilian was killed and another wounded in the crossfire. The explosive blew up part of the station, but only one SAS member and the RUC constable were injured. All eight terrorists, on the other hand, were killed. The result was a massive loss of prestige for the IRA, a loss that caused them to search for a new high-profile target.

One of the targets they chose was the Changing of the Guard ceremony on Gibraltar, where regiments were often rotated after leaving Ulster. Based on MI5 intelligence that an attack on the Royal Anglian Regiment's band on

Gibraltar was imminent, an SAS team flew there March 3, 1988. The team included at least one bomb disposal expert and six well-trained "shooters." On March 6, the SAS surveillance team was following the three primary IRA terrorists who had been identified—terrorists with lengthy records of committing violence against innocent civilians. When the IRA members spotted the surveillance, they reacted as though they were going to use a radio-controlled device to detonate the explosives the SAS team had been led to believe were in a parked automobile. The SAS immediately opened fire, shooting until the terrorists were dead. Although known to be hardened members of an IRA Active Service Unit, the three were unarmed and did not have a detonating device. The fact that one was a woman added to public outcry about the killings. Arising once again were accusations that the SAS was pursuing a "shoot to kill" policy against the IRA. The SAS took substantial criticism in the liberal press, although the

Member of the French SAS operating in occupied Europe in support of the French Resistance during World War II. ECP

shootings were eventually ruled in court to be justified. The SAS had abided by the rules of engagement under which they were operating: Official control had passed from the Gibraltar police to the SAS commander on the scene; their initial aim was to arrest the terrorists, and they had fired only to defend lives. Much was made in the press accounts of the number of rounds fired by the SAS, but since the nature of the threat was such that they had to be sure the terrorists could not initiate a remote-control firing device, firing had to continue until the terrorists were immobilized.

Gibraltar marked the first time that the SAS's campaign against the IRA had moved outside of the United Kingdom itself, but it was only the latest of a long line of SAS counter-ambushes against IRA Active Service Units intent on mayhem. The SAS remains an actual and a psychological check on the IRA. The facts that the SAS has stopped numerous IRA operations and that the IRA is especially paranoid about the SAS act as a counter to IRA operations. Therefore, as long as the British Army and intelligence agencies remain committed in Ulster, it is likely that there will remain some SAS commitment as well.

The South Atlantic War

On April 2, 1982, D Squadron of 22nd SAS Regiment went on three hour alert after the Argentine invasion of the Falklands. Although the SAS Operational Intelligence Unit, the "Kremlin," had intelligence available for all types of likely deployments for the SAS, there were no contingency plans for the Falkland Islands, a fact that bore out the validity of training Special Forces Troops to expect the unexpected. Nevertheless, D Squadron was sent to Ascension Island to join the task force headed for the South Atlantic.

The first mission assigned to D Squadron was assisting in the re-conquest of South Georgia; hence, D Squadron embarked on the fleet auxiliary *Fort Austin*. Also assigned to the South Georgia Task Force was a Royal Marine Company and about twenty-five SBS members. After arriving off South Georgia, D Squadron's

SAS men often used captured German weapons. This suppressed CZ27, for example, was used by an SAS man who had taken it from one of Otto Skorzeny's operatives. Pete Mason

Mountain Troop was assigned to land north of Leith for a recce. The SBS was also to be landed southeast of Grytviken, South Georgia's main settlement. Once ashore, both units would establish observation posts and gather intelligence about the Argentine garrison. Mountain Troop's attempt to land on Fortuna Glacier was launched on April 21 in wind-driven snow. Visibility was so bad that it took the helicopters inserting the troop three attempts to land. Conditions grew even worse during the night, increasing the threat of hypothermia and frostbite. As a result, the next day, three Wessex helicopters attempted to extract the soldiers, but one crashed in the heavy snow. Those who had been

aboard this chopper were picked up by the other two, but one of those then crashed as well. The surviving Wessex managed to make it back to the ship, returning later that evening to pull the remaining SAS and helicopter crew out.

After a day of considering the options for inserting another party, on April 23, D Squadron's Boat Troop took off in five three-man inflatables. Only two of the inflatables' motors were working, however, so these towed the three others. During the approach to Grass Island, where the expected landing site was located, two of those inflatables being towed broke loose and were swept away. The other three did manage to make it ashore and set up their ob-

An SAS Jeep Patrol of the type that operated behind German lines in Europe. IWM

Falklands more rapidly. As a result, from May 1 on, SAS parties kept watch on Argentine garrisons around Stanley and elsewhere. After arriving in the Falklands after the South Georgia operations, D Squadron was also used on reconnaissance missions. Often, these small parties were inserted at night via the limited helicopter lift available to the task force. Normally, the patrols would be inserted far away from their objective. Then, covering a maximum of 15km at night while avoiding Argentine campfires, they would move to the sites where they established their observation posts. One of the most useful of these posts overlooked Port Stanley from Beaver Ridge. From this post, the SAS spotted Argentine helicopters being redeployed and guided Harriers in to destroy them. Although the observation posts were highly effective, some SAS patrols had to occupy them for up to four weeks, only able to move outside for short periods at night.

In addition to providing invaluable intelligence, the SAS also conducted carrying out three major raids in the Falklands. The first of these was on Pebble Island to destroy Argentine aircraft that could have been used against the landings at San Carlos. Realizing how vulnerable the landings would be, British commanders wanted to take every precaution to counter Argentine air power possible. Boat Troop of D Squadron, the same personnel who had landed on South Georgia, carried out the initial reconnaissance of the airstrip on May 13. Then, on May 15, the raid was launched, with one troop assigned to hit the planes with LAWs and small arms, and another troop assigned to seal the approaches to the airstrip. A third troop remained in reserve. An 81mm mortar and explosive charges were also taken along. After being inserted by helicopter, the raiders covered 6km from their landing zone to the airstrip. A barrage from the 81mm mortar and naval gunfire helped keep the defenders pinned down while

servation posts to watch the whaling stations at Leith and Stormness. Bad weather caused the SBS teams to abort their reconnaissance mission as well. The next morning the crew of one of the inflatables was rescued, although at this point the other remained missing.

The SBS teams were eventually re-inserted and an Argentine submarine was attacked in Cumberland Bay, thus revealing the British presence and forcing a mixed SAS and Royal Marine team to retake the whaling stations. With naval gunfire support available, the SAS and Royal Marines took the Argentine surrender. Adding to the jubilation was the fact that the next morning, the inflatable crew still missing was found and rescued. Although the Mountain and Boat Troops had found the conditions under which they were operating severe, the selection and training procedure proved effective, as all managed to survive and/or carry out their missions.

G Squadron had also been sent south toward the Falklands for intelligence-gathering missions. At least some SAS troops had, in fact, carried out a wet jump and been picked up by *H.M.S. Andromeda* to enable them to reach the

Territorial Army SAS men on patrol in Scandinavia illustrate that all-around security must be maintained on patrol. Special Air Service

Weapons with special optics often proved invaluable during operations in the Falklands, where the SAS and SBS could move undetected only at night. IWM

the raiders attached explosive charges to Pucara ground support aircraft, fuel supplies, and the ammunition dump. All eleven aircraft were destroyed, with only one SAS injury. Paddy Mayne's ghost, no doubt, watched the proceedings with proper appreciation.

Another raiding assignment fell to D Squadron on the night of the landings when a diversion was called for. The squadron lost eighteen men in a helicopter accident while shifting personnel between ships, but those remaining raided Darwin with machine guns, mortars, MILANs, and rifles. During the attack, one trooper also shot down a Pucara with a Stinger anti-aircraft missile. This was the only real success for the Stinger, which members of the SAS who had been training in the United States brought with them. However, the soldier most highly trained in their use had been lost in the helicopter crash, which may have explained the lack of success.

For the next two weeks, the SAS carried out ambushes and patrols, especially around Mount

For certain operations, such as those in the Falklands, the SAS is inserted from carriers by the Royal Navy. IWM

Kent, which the SAS held virtually alone for five days. Five patrols were also landed on West Falkland on June 5. On one recce near Berkeley Sound, an SAS and SBS patrol bumped into each other and got into a firefight, a continuing danger when multiple special operations units are operating in an area. Another SAS officer was killed while directing naval gunfire and his radioman was captured.

Lieutenant Colonel Mike Rose had been in touch with Argentine headquarters on East Falkland, where he had been attempting a bit of psychological operations with the help of a Spanish-speaking Royal Marine officer. Later, Rose participated in the surrender negotiations and relayed news of the surrender to London via the SAS satellite communications system.

Before the surrender, however, on the night of June 13–14, SAS and SBS teams raided the oil storage tanks in Stanley Harbor. They approached in small boats, but the Argentine defenses proved too strong for them to complete the raid. Nevertheless, the attempt helped convince the Argentines that the British would be able to raid virtually at will. In more clandestine operations, SAS patrols reportedly landed on the Argentine mainland to report on aircraft deployments, although this may have been a bit of psychological operations as well. In any case, a British helicopter did crash under odd circumstances just across the Chilean border with Argentina.

Once again, the Falklands War proved a good example of the SAS's ability to rapidly deploy anywhere in the world and carry out reconnaissance and raids successfully.

Among the many problems faced by SAS patrols in the Falklands were the large number of Argentine mines planted around Argie positions. IWM

Chapter 6

Counterterrorism, Executive Protection, and Hostage Rescue

The SAS actually got involved in counterterrorism through the back door, but then back doors are often excellent points of entry for counterterrorist units. To a large extent, SAS members have traditionally been trained to function as official terrorists, destabilizing and creating confusion for the enemy. Being the United Kingdom's principal counterinsurgency force as well, the SAS has, of necessity, learned to deal with various aspects of urban guerrilla warfare, and many of the same techniques have carried over to their counterterrorist missions. One of the earliest SAS involvements in what is now considered counterterrorism came through the teams provided by the SAS to train the bodyguards of foreign leaders. In a few cases—most notably, the Sultan of Oman—the SAS has even provided protective teams. Interestingly, in a classified Ministry of Defense film intended to orient members of other regiments to SAS capabilities, the sequence on close-protection teams shows a group of SAS men guarding what is obviously a Middle Eastern head of state. The SAS has on occasion, however, reinforced the close-protection teams provided by Scotland Yard to members of the royal family as well, especially during visits outside of Great Britain.

The late 1960s also saw the SAS assign a

SAS Counterrevolutionary Warfare assault gear, circa 1980, includes antiflash hood, gas mask, ballistic vest, H&K MP5, Browning Hi-Power, and spare MP5 mag pouch. Note the spare Hi-Power magazine on the wrist for fast access. Ken MacSwan illustration

unit to study terrorism, particularly aircraft or ship hijackers, and to develop tactics to counter them. The unit also studied the best ways to carry out such hijackings. The earliest SAS units also were deployed to Northern Ireland at about this time, necessitating that the regiment begin working on techniques to rapidly clear urban buildings containing both hostile terrorists and innocent civilians.

After the Munich Massacre of Israeli Olympic athletes graphically illustrated the vulnerability of the Western democracies to terrorism, the SAS began to devote more personnel and study to the counterterrorist mission. By the mid-1970s, a full squadron was assigned on rotation. The SAS did not automatically become a top hostage rescue unit overnight, however. Members of the earliest Special Projects Team remember attempting many tactics that proved complete failures, but hard work and detailed analysis of why something didn't work have always been SAS strong points, and the troopers assigned to counterterrorism continually improved. Over the years, the SAS took advantage of its contacts with other hostage rescue units, too. SAS members were present, for example, when the Royal Dutch Marines assaulted the Depunt train in 1977 and again in 1978, going in with GSG-9 to deploy stun grenades during the assault on a hijacked airliner at Mogadishu. During these operations, the SAS offered their own expertise and took the knowledge they had gained back to Hereford. After the Depunt train assault, for example, the SAS spent months perfecting their own techniques for assaulting a train.

Rotating squadrons through the counterterrorist assignment has proven to have many advantages. It helps the soldiers maintain the edge necessary to train for months or even years for an operation that may last for only minutes, and it ensures that wherever an SAS squadron is deployed, there will be a counterterrorist capability. Generally, the Counter Revolutionary Warfare Squadron, known within the SAS as the SP Team, is somewhat overstrength, with about seventy-eight personnel assigned.

As with other SAS Sabre Squadrons, the CRW Squadron is normally broken into four operational troops, each of sixteen men. The basic operational unit remains the four- man patrol. Each troop is divided somewhat differently for CRW deployment, however. There will be a containment group consisting of snipers and surveillance experts and an assault group. Generally, most members of a troop can perform multiple functions, although certain men make better snipers. The SAS Operations Research Unit has developed many special devices for the SP Teams, perhaps the best known of which is the

An SAS instructor discusses with US Army personnel deployment of gas before an entry.

"stun grenade." Additionally, special assault ladders and light mounts for weapons, as well as other useful items, have been created to let the assault teams get into a building and neutralize the situation faster or to gather more accurate intelligence about the area before an assault. Many items used on other SAS operations, such as thermal imagers, are supplemented by more specialized surveillance items, such as endoscopes to insert a wide-angle fiber optic lens through a pinhole without detection. Standard SAS vehicles are also supplemented with special vans with ladders mounted atop them via hinges to allow a rapid second-story entry. As with most equipment, the SAS goes for practicality above all else with their CRW gear.

Another advantage the SAS has had in training squadrons to function as hostage rescuers is that many of the skills taught to such units are already within the capabilities of SAS soldiers. Hand-to-hand combat, marksmanship, parachuting, scuba, mountaineering, communications, demolitions, teamwork, building clearing—all skills that many hostage rescue units have to learn after selection—are already within the squadron's realm of expertise before it even begins specialized counterterrorist training. The SAS, in fact, views CRW skills as just another of the many useful pieces of arcane knowledge which combine to make the successful SAS long-term enlisted soldier. The SAS also manages to combine some of the odd chores it is asked to perform, such as testing prison security or armed vehicle security, with their counterterrorist training. Having tested the security of many of the United Kingdom's prisons, for example, should the SAS be called to deal with a prison riot, many members of the unit will be quite familiar with the prison, having "broken out of it" a time or two. One supposedly escape-proof prison, by the way, held its SAS evaluators for only a matter of minutes.

One of the most critical skills for those assigned to the counterterrorist squadron is close-quarters battle (CQB). In simple terms, CQB is the ability to rapidly and effectively neutralize an enemy at close range, particularly with small arms. In the SAS "Killing House," a shooting fa-

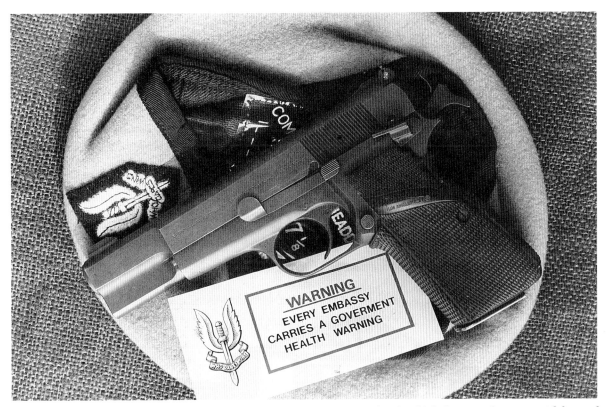

A little bit of SAS humor after the rescue at "Princess Gate" along with the Browning Hi-Power, which, due to its use by the SAS, became the most widely used handgun among counterterrorist units.

cility designed to simulate scenarios likely to be encountered when clearing a building, the SAS hones the already highly developed marksmanship ability of trainees through a six-week CQB shooting course using 1,200 to 1,500 rounds. Six rooms were available in the original "Killing House," allowing for various scenarios. Once this basic CQB course has been completed, skills will be honed even more for those on the SP Team through constant live-fire drills. More sophisticated techniques, such as shooting on the move and in tactical positions, are combined with rapid magazine changes and malfunction clearance drills. Rapid placement of multiple hits on targets, often in the head, and instantaneous target acquisition, especially in low light, are practiced until those assigned the SAS

counterterrorist mission are quick and deadly combat shooters. To make scenarios as realistic as possible, members of the SP Team and/or their instructors often act as hostages so that in a crisis entry, each man has placed and can place again a shot within inches of a hostage to take out the terrorist. Traditionally, the SAS has taught double taps with the pistol and three shot bursts with the "Hockler" submachine gun, but more recently emphasis has been on shooting until the target is stopped.

Recently, there have been some changes in the use of live hostages as well. After one man died in such realistic training, a loss mourned but considered necessary within the Regiment to keep troops and hostages alive during a real assault, the new "Killing House" at Sterling

Lines was redesigned so that live hostages and terrorists are in a separate room from the one the team practicing entries will actually enter. Through closed-circuit video, however, actions of the "hostages" and "terrorists" are projected realistically into the room being entered. Since this system allows the entry to be taped and critiqued, most members of the SAS not only

US Army hostage rescue personnel under the training of the author and SAS instructors learn techniques for clearing a bus that has been hijacked. Among the points to notice are that entry is carried out from multiple points and that some personnel control the interior of the bus via the windows. The key assault elements, however, enter through either the front or back, with one MP5-armed man controlling one side of the bus, while others clear the aisles.

*Members of a US Army counterterrorist unit practice
SAS-style bus assaults*

find it safer but also more effective as a training device.

The SAS also tries to vary scenarios to fit likely targets, including trains, planes, ships, and buildings. In many cases, British Airways jets are used for training, as are the QE II; and various trains, reportedly even the Orient Express. Buildings ranging from the Bank of England to Buckingham Palace to the Houses of Parliament have hosted SAS survey teams preparing for the time when they might have to be "taken down." These surveys are often fed into an extensive computer database maintained by the SAS Operational Intelligence Unit. In addition to providing information, the SAS computer system can suggest possible assault tactics to fit a situation, although with the long-standing SAS tradition of critical evalua-

tion, such programs will certainly not be blindly followed but will be viewed as just one additional tool for planning an operation.

Exchanges with other counterterrorist units also keep the SP Team sharp and help their members learn additional skills. West Germany's GSG-9 and the United States' Delta Force and FBI HRT are among those with whom the SAS trains most frequently. Occasionally, such cross-training makes for interesting exchanges, due to language differences. During one joint training session with Delta, for example, SAS members were acting as the terrorists while a group of American female soldiers were included among the hostages. When the negotiator failed to meet the terrorist's demands, one of the SAS terrorists dragged a female hostage to the window and shouted, "OK, that's it; I'm going to give her a head job!" In SAS slang, this means a shot to the head, but the nonplused "hostage," of course, assumed he meant the American slang version.

Other Western counterterrorist units, including the Royal Dutch Marines, France's GIGN, Spain's GEO, and Canada's RCMP ERTs and, more recently, Special Service Force, have carried out training with the SAS as well. The Israelis, on the other hand, have not. From the days when Palestine was a British protectorate, there is still a deep-seated distrust among SAS members for the Israelis, stemming to a large extent from the fact that a Jewish bomb intended for legendary SAS man Roy Farran, who had operated undercover squads in Palestine, killed his brother instead. Members of the SAS have a long

US Army hostage rescue personnel undergoing room clearing training under SAS instruction.

US Army hostage rescue team member learning instinctive use of the MP5 under instruction from SAS instructors.

institutional memory. Exchanges of information do take place informally, however, through GSG-9, which maintains good relations with both the SAS and Israel's Border Police counterterrorist unit. Instances where the SAS actually participated in operations by other hostage rescue units have already been discussed, but there are numerous other instances where one or two SAS members were present, although their involvement has been kept hidden.

Part of being a member of the Sabre Squadron on CRW duty is remaining ready for instant deployment anywhere in the world where British citizens may be threatened. As a result, the members of the alert portion of the squadron will wear beepers when away from Sterling Lines, and standard callback codes are in effect for those members visiting one of the two or three pubs around Hereford favored by SAS men. Usually, these callbacks consist of something as simple as paging a nonexistent person in the pub. With the advent of beepers, however, this system is normally not used today. At nearby RAF Lyneham, a C-130 is on standby, 24 hours a day, 365 days a year, to take the CRW Squadron into action.

Although the Operations Research Unit is always on the lookout for special weapons and equipment, much of the hardware used by the SAS is fairly standard. Members of the assault teams wear Nomex suits reinforced with Kevlar at the knees and elbows (as these joints usually take the worst beatings going through doors and windows rapidly). Although the gray anti-flash hoods worn in earlier operations became something of an SAS trademark, ballistic helmets and Armorshield body armor are now worn during entries. Gas masks—"respirators" in British Army terminology—are worn during assaults for several reasons: The assault teams will already be prepared should it prove tactically useful to deploy CS gas, and the masks give the assault teams a psychological advantage as well as a fierce (but, to other team members, quickly recognizable) appearance.

The SAS rappelling harness—"abseiling harness" in British Army terminology—includes a leg bag for the rope so that it cannot drop down past a window and reveal the approaching entry. Most recent communication equipment has been the Davis CT100 radio system, which filters out gunshots and explosions as well as other loud noises likely to be present during an assault but allows easy voice communication among members of the teams. Stun grenades are carried on the strong-side (dominant hand side) thigh, while three spare magazines for the MP5 submachine gun are carried in a weak-side hip pouch. Two spare pistol magazines are carried on the weak-side thigh and a third spare is sometimes strapped onto the strong-side wrist for rapid access.

The SAS used the Browning Hi-Power from World War II until a couple of years ago when the Operations Research Unit determined that a double-action automatic would be more effective for SAS members on assignments where they were armed in street clothes and had to quickly bring their weapons into action. As a result, the SIG P-226/228 has been adopted. The Hi-Power was normally carried with an extension magazine in place to give added firepower, and this seems to be the case with the SIG as well.

Originally, the SP Teams were armed with MAC M-10 submachine guns, but after the Mo-gadishu operation, those SAS men who had accompanied GSG-9 were so impressed with the H&K MP5 that it was adopted by the SAS as well. The "Hockler" fires from a closed bolt, which gives it excellent accuracy, one of the reasons the SAS has found it so effective for hostage rescue operations. The standard shotgun has been the Remington 870, used primarily for taking hinges off of doors during rapid entries. SAS sniper rifles have been discussed previously, but to recap, for counterterrorist operations, the basic rifle is the Accuracy International PM, the L96A1 in military designation. Chambered for the 7.62mm NATO round, the L96A1 is fitted with a Schmidt and Bender PM 6x42 scope. The SAS considers the L96A1 effective for shots out to 300m or longer, although they also have available a .300 Magnum version for even longer shots. For shorter-range urban sniping, there is also a .243 version, which the SAS calls their "soft kill rifle." A suppressed rifle is their "quiet kill" weapon.

Other units have adopted the SAS philosophy that the more realistic the training, the more likely the chances of survival. Here are US Army personnel practicing SAS entry and room clearing tactics.

SAS deployments with GSG-9 and the Royal Dutch Marines have already been mentioned, but the counterterrorist teams have been deployed for operations affecting British interests as well. The first such deployment is generally considered to be a wet jump by members of the SAS and SBS to join the *Queen Elizabeth II* at sea when there had been a bomb threat. No explosive device was dis-covered, but the availability of airborne/scuba/de-molitions-trained personnel in the two units allowed this fact to be determined quickly without having to turn the ship around. In January 1975, an Iranian passenger hijacked an airliner from Manchester. Although he ordered the pilot to fly to Paris, after being flown around a bit, he was landed at an airport in Essex, where the SAS

SAS training attempts to incorporate as much realism as possible. This humanoid target invented by a former SAS man, for example, uses a balloon inside of the "head." If a proper head shot is scored, the target will "die" and fall down; if not, the training operation is a failure.

Just as these US Army hostage rescue personnel incorporate a shotgunner to blow door hinges, so do the SAS. The shotgunner can also act as rear security man.

S normally uses a four-man entry ele-
...rmy personnel are learning SAS tac-
...heir five-man element.

During hostage rescue operations, entries may have to be carried out from above to retain stealth.

awaited him. He was taken alive and handed over to police. The early SAS SP Teams were also rushed to the airport to prevent Idi Amin from landing to pay an official visit, but as it turned out, their presence was not needed. December 1975 saw a callout as well when an IRA Active Service Unit was barricaded in Balcombe Street in London. The announcement over the radio that the SAS had arrived was enough to play on the traditional IRA paranoia about the SAS, and the gunmen surrendered.

The most famous SAS counterterrorist employment also came in London on May 5, 1980, when Pagoda Troop assaulted the Iranian Embassy to end a six-day siege. The embassy

takeover had begun on April 30, when a group opposed to the Khomeni government and seeking independence for Arabistan had seized the embassy along with twenty-six hostages, including a British newscameraman and a policeman from the Diplomatic Protection Group. The terrorists were armed with two submachine guns, four handguns, and grenades. Five of the hostages were released quite early in the ordeal due to medical problems and provided some early intelligence about what was going on inside the embassy.

Police Constable Lock had managed to radio an alert before he was taken hostage; hence, the Metropolitan Police's D11 Unit had taken up

SAS policy and that of most counterterrorist units is to assign multiple snipers to each target. This allows for a more absolute certainty of kill and also allows each sniper to rest awhile without leaving the target uncovered.

Snipers may be deployed in hostage rescue situations both to gain intelligence and to solve the problem at long range. This sniper from one of the Spanish coun-terterrorist units has received training quite similar to that of SAS snipers.

sniper/countersniper positions, while C13, the Metropolitan Police's Antiterrorist Squad, and C7, the Technical Support Branch, had moved into position as well. C7's primary job was to set up command posts and surveillance. The SAS alert team beepers went off as many of the men were practicing CQB in the regiment's "Killing House." A former member of the SAS serving as a dog handler with the Metropolitan Police had put in a call to Hereford to give the SP Team early warning that they were likely to be needed. Much of the SP Team's specialized equipment is prepacked and ready for immediate departure, thus speeding their deployment to London.

The alert team—Pagoda Troop—was deployed to London, initially to a barracks in Regents Park. Intelligence gathering began early as SAS intelligence experts in civilian clothes carried out reconnaissance around the embassy.

Among the many units that have incorporated SAS techniques into their training are these US Army Rangers. 75th Rangers

The SAS has a well-developed procedure for rapidly gathering intelligence at the site of a hostage incident, much of it based on checklists developed in advance. Such rapid intelligence gathering is critical, as an immediate action plan has to be developed in case the terrorists start killing hostages. Such plans are usually relatively unsophisticated at the beginning but evolve as more information becomes available. As an assault appeared likely, members of the SP Team carried out recces on the roof of the embassy as well. At a little-used London barracks, members of the assault teams practiced their assault drills, the plan evolving as more

information about the embassy was gained. Initial plans called for the teams to break through ground-level windows with sledgehammers, but fortunately, a caretaker for the embassy provided invaluable intelligence, including the fact that the windows were armored. The plan was adjusted and frame charges to blow windows

Members of the Special Air Service counterterrorist team practice train entries. After members of the SAS were present during the Depunt train assault by the Royal Dutch Marines, the SAS put great stress on such operations. Special Air Service

106

were constructed. A model of the more than fifty rooms making up the embassy was also constructed and intensively studied. Additionally, microphones were reportedly suspended down the chimney in an attempt to gain information about where the hostages were being held.

The negotiators from the Metropolitan Police were also invaluable sources of intelligence as negotiations dragged on. The negotiators did get the terrorists to drop their demand that prisoners in Iran be freed, but they continued to demand mediators from a friendly Arab state. As the British government was unwilling to grant safe conduct to the terrorists, the negotiators were really attempting to stall for time and to wear the terrorists down. By May 5, though,

the terrorists were becoming frustrated, and it became apparent to the negotiators that the hostages were in danger. The SAS had been moved closer in case it was necessary to send them in, and the landing pattern for planes approaching London had been slightly changed to increase the noise level around the embassy to help cover movement if the assault team had to get into position. This, by the way, has since become a rather standard tactic; jackhammers later being used to cover the assault in Italy to rescue General Dozier, for example. Three shots were heard at 1331 and another three at 1850. After the latter group of shots, a body of one of the hostages was rolled out the door and the terrorist leader said it would be followed by anoth-

Members of Pagoda Troop prepare to rappel down from the top of the Iranian embassy in London. Note the sledgehammers carried for entry. Special Air Service

er dead body in 45min. As police negotiators began stalling to prevent more killings, the SAS teams prepared to go in. While the negotiator asked the terrorist leader how large a bus they would need to go to the airport, the SAS assault teams were counting down the seconds prior to their entry.

"Operation Nimrod" began at 1923 as eight SAS men rappelled from the embassy roof to the first-floor balcony and ground-floor terrace at the rear of the embassy. Operating in two-man units, they prepared the frame charges to blow the windows to gain entry. A member of the assault group, one of the Fijian SAS men, got entangled in his rope during his descent, and his legs were burned during the entry.

The windows breached, the teams threw in stun grenades and began clearing the embassy.

Members of Pagoda Troop prepare to go through the windows, which have just been blown, of the Iranian *embassy in London. Note the flashlights mounted above the MP5s.* Special Air Service

Members of Pagoda Troop carry out the entry at "Princess Gate." Special Air Service

Reportedly, the first team found itself in a room they had thought contained hostages but which proved to be empty. Egress from this room was also reportedly blocked, slowing the assault slightly. As soon as possible, however, this group headed for the telex room, where most of the hostages were known to be held. The terrorist leader had been on the phone with negotiators as the assault began. Spotting a member of the assault force coming through a window, he prepared to fire on him. Constable Lock, however, tackled the terrorist, and then rolled aside so that the SAS man could kill him.

While the first group was gaining entry, another four-man group had entered through the second-floor window after reaching the balcony from adjoining buildings. They followed their stun grenades through the window and began clearing the building as well, in many cases shooting the locks out of doors with their MP5s to speed entry. Still another party reportedly burst through the plaster at a point which had been previously weakened. The primary objective remained the telex room, where fifteen male hostages were held. Before the SAS could reach the telex room, two terrorists there killed one hostage and wounded two, but before they could continue killing, they were killed by a barrage of 9mm bullets from MP5s. A third terrorist in this room mingled with the hostages and survived as a result.

To quickly clear the embassy in case it was wired with explosives, the teams rushed the hostages down the stairs and outside. One terrorist coming down with the hostages was spotted with a grenade and butt-stroked with an MP5, then riddled with bullets when he rolled clear. As the hostages were thrown outside, they were secured on the ground to make sure none had fallen prey to the "Stockholm Syndrome" and were aiding the terrorists or that none were terrorists or unknown confederates of the terrorists. The one terrorist who survived the assault had been the youngest one who had mingled with the women hostages who were protecting him . The entire operations from start to final evacuation of SAS personnel from the building had taken only about 11min.

Teams undergoing bodyguard training learn to deal with an ambush involving fire and explosives.

Although the SAS had avoided publicity for years, the "Princess Gate" rescue took place on national television. There were advantages to this, however, as a graphic message was sent to terrorists contemplating acts against Great Britain: the SAS will kill you! The operation also showed the validity and the viability of the long hours of live-fire practice and the expenditure of substantial sums of money in training the counterterrorist unit of the SAS. As with most counterterrorist operations, the assault plan had to be adjusted as it was carried out, and the flexibility of SAS training prepared the men carrying out the assault to deal with the pressure and the difficulty of the operation. The SAS had also illustrated a truism most of those who are involved in counterterrorism are aware of: Dead terrorists are far better than live terrorists in prisons. Live terrorists are magnets for further terrorist acts to free them.

Subsequent SAS counterterrorist deployments have included breaking a prison siege and deployment to a London embassy again, this time when members of the Libyan delegation fired shots into a crowd, killing a British policewoman. Others remain classified. Most importantly, as this is written, around Here-

The SAS maintains many specialized weapons in their armory, such as these two suppressed automatics of the type used by the Israeli Mossad. Pete Mason

ford, a few dozen men are on alert ready to "Dare to Win" the freedom of British hostages. The knowledge that the highly professional and skilled SAS counterterrorist team was ready to go into action has, no doubt, deterred numerous acts against British citizens and will continue to do so in the future.

Before ending the discussion of SAS counterterrorist capabilities, their training in VIP protection should also be mentioned. Often the best bodyguards are those who are trained themselves to carry out snatches or assassinations, and SAS bodyguards are no exceptions. Close-protection training has been carried out by the SAS for more than two decades and substantial expertise has been developed. Many of the security agencies employing former mem-

bers of the SAS, in fact, specialize in providing bodyguards. The SAS still occasionally provides bodyguards to high-threat members of the government, particularly the Prime Minister or the Royal Family, during certain official visits where the normal one- to three-man or woman protective team from Scotland Yard is not considered sufficient. But many close-protection assignments formerly carried out by members of the SAS are now carried out by members of the Royal Military Police, who receive quite comprehensive executive protection training based on a syllabus originally developed by the SAS.

Many of the specialized skills members of the SAS learn during close-protection training have other applications, such as vehicle counterambush tactics for when they are riding in an automobile that comes under attack. Many of these same tactics, for example, may be applied in Northern Ireland. Explosive recces, in which members of the regiment learn to check vehicles or buildings for Improvised Explosive Devices have had good carry-over to service in Northern Ireland or other assignments. The fact that members of the SAS are trained to make good use of such devices themselves is an aid in carrying out explosive recces as well, since most SAS members look first in the place they would have planted a booby trap! Foot-and-vehicle escort formations for moving a VIP through crowds or into and out of vehicles and buildings are practiced until they can be done with well-oiled precision. Use of advance teams to prepare

Close-protection personnel undergoing training under instruction from former members of the SAS, including the "VIP" here being evacuated.

During high-threat executive protection training, SAS members learn to cover and evacuate the VIP while those closest to the attack counter it. Members of an

executive protection team undergoing training in SAS debus techniques. Note that one man covers to rear to prevent the group from being flanked.

113

*Counterambush training includes learning to proper-
ly use the engine compartment and wheel wells for
cover.*

*Another clandestine method for carrying the MP5
ready for action.*

for a VIP visit, emergency medical techniques
applicable to trauma, high-speed and evasive
driving, countersurveillance, and numerous other somewhat esoteric skills are normally
learned as part of preparation for close-protection training.

Operating in the close-protection and the
counterterrorist role, small teams of SAS men
are often deployed to British embassies, particularly those considered most vulnerable to attack. They have also provided close-protection
for allies of Great Britain, the regiment's reputation often making such protection a particu-
lar status symbol among visiting third-world
royals.

Close-protection team learning SAS debus under fire and counterambush tactics.

On some clandestine or low-profile operations, members of the SAS must keep their MP5s hidden. When guarding the Royal Family in certain high-threat situations, for example, this carrier might be used.

Among specialized training given to many SAS men is offensive and defensive driving. Ambush and counterambush skills are also taught to members of the SAS. In this case, the debus under fire is being practiced.

Chapter 7

The SAS for Export

Rhodesian SAS and Selous Scouts

During the counterinsurgency campaign in Malaya, "Mad Mike" Calvert traveled to Rhodesia in search of recruits for the resurgent SAS and found 1,000 fit and willing volunteers. From these, the best 100 were selected to form C Squadron of the SAS. Many Rhodesians had served with the Long-Range Desert Group and at least one had later joined the SAS in the desert. Along with the remainder of the SAS, C Squadron underwent six weeks of intensive jungle training in Malaya, where they were joined by Lieutenant Peter Walls, who was quickly promoted to captain when given command of the squadron. Later, as commander of Rhodesia's Security Forces during the Rhodesian counterinsurgency war, Walls got a chance to apply much of what he had learned in Malaya. Walls' experience as an SAS officer also allowed him to appreciate the value of special operations units such as the Selous Scouts and Rhodesian SAS. Another one of these early Rhodesian recruits was Ron Reid-Daly, who would later command the Selous Scouts.

Original plans had called for a British officer to command C Squadron, but despite his youth, Walls was made an acting major and given permanent command of the squadron. While serving in Malaya, virtually all members of C Squadron eventually underwent parachute

Maori member of the New Zealand SAS on operations in Vietnam. New Zealand SAS

training. During their two-year tour, they also learned counterinsurgency operations, jungle tracking, and ambush/counterambush.

Upon their return from Malaya (where three men had been killed in action) C Squadron was disbanded, but when Rhodesia decided to form a parachute unit in 1961, the squadron was reformed. Recruitment for the new unit was carried out in Rhodesia, the United Kingdom, and South Africa. Once the initial nucleus had been selected, they were sent to Hereford to train with 22nd SAS and to do a basic parachute course. Once this group returned to Rhodesia, it was decided that their ranks would be expanded to 184 men, including troops and support personnel. The first selection course took place in the Matapas Mountain Range and was generally conceded to be as tough as that of the parent unit back in the United Kingdom. An early accomplishment of those who had received their parachute training in the United Kingdom was the establishment of the first Rhodesian parachute school near Salisbury in October 1961.

In 1962, C Squadron joined elements of the British SAS for exercises in Aden, followed later in the year by their first operational jump on an internal security mission in Rhodesia. 1962 saw the unit training on helicopters to develop basic airmobile tactics. Finally, late in that year, the SAS was deployed along the border near Ndola between Zambia and the Congo to make sure the war there didn't spill over. In at least one case, a member of C Squadron spilled

Members of the Australian SAS on patrol. Australian SAS

over into the war, as John Peters, an Englishman who had joined the Rhodesian SAS, would eventually command the mercenary 5 Commando in the Congo after Mike Hoare had left. When Northern Rhodesia was given its independence as Zambia and Malawi, only thirty-one members of C Squadron chose to return to Southern Rhodesia.

In 1963, the first Rhodesian soldier killed in the counterinsurgency war was a member of C Squadron. In addition to being engaged in internal security operations, however, C Squadron wondered, as relations worsened with Great Britain, if they might find themselves in combat against the British Army. As a result of intensive recruiting throughout the world, C Squadron's strength was brought back to near its authorized numbers by the Unilateral Declaration of Independence of November 1965. Her Majesty's Government did not respond militarily, but C Squadron found itself facing an ever more intensive counterinsurgency throughout

the later 1960s. As a result, the unit was almost constantly in the bush, either hunting men or beasts. Such a large proportion of the members of the Rhodesian SAS had worked as "White Hunters," in fact, that the unit was sometimes known as "Special Air Safaris." "White" hunters would be especially appropriate, too, as the SAS remained an all-white unit until Rhodesia was negotiated out of existence.

In addition to being committed to internal operations, during 1967, members of C Squadron fought with the Portuguese against Communist guerrillas in Angola. Although it has not been widely publicized, C Squadron's services were offered to the United States, as well, for use in Vietnam since the Rhodesians considered any anti-Communist war a good war. Of course, they hoped that such an offer would win the United States' support in their own counterinsurgency campaign. With a large black minority, the United States could not, however, accept the Rhodesian offer, although Australian and

New Zealand SAS troops would serve alongside US personnel in Vietnam.

As it turned out, there was plenty of action for C Squadron in Rhodesia. By the early 1970s, C Squadron was serving as a quick-reaction force that could be dropped by parachute to cut off terrorists fleeing back to Zambia or Mozambique after incursions into Rhodesia. This mission would later become a specialty of the Rhodesian Light Infantry when it became airborne-qualified so that the SAS could be freed for more typically special forces' missions. For example, cross-border strikes—first into Mozambique and later into Zambia—hit terrorist infiltration routes and base camps. Insertions for these missions were often via HALO directly onto terrorist camps. Other missions were inserted via helicopter or Land Rovers painted in the camouflage scheme of the country in which they were operating. Still other cross-border operations were inserted via a parachute jump some distance from the target, followed by a night march to the objective. During such operations, bridges were destroyed, guerrilla camps raided, and guerrilla leaders "neutralized."

Many operations were also carried out across the Zambesi River using Klepper canoes, Zodiac rubber boats, or other small craft. SAS patrols along the river also kept a sharp eye for hollow logs floating across the river with terrorists inside, a common infiltration method. In fact, floating logs were often used for target practice as a double precaution, although obviously not when on a clandestine operation.

In the tradition of SAS operations everywhere, C Squadron found that small patrols could inflict the maximum amount of destruction, death, and disorientation on the terrorists. Among patrol missions were sabotage, reconnaissance, and booby trapping of terrorist trail networks. Because so many of the SAS men were professional hunters, they even developed the standard operating procedure of urinating around booby traps so that game animals would stay away and not set them off.

During the counterinsurgency war, SAS selection remained rigorous. It began with a 36–48-hour marathon requiring constant exertion without sleep. Those surviving this phase began a twenty-mile endurance march carrying a pack and rifle. Other long, forced marches followed over the next two weeks. Selection completed, those remaining began their actual SAS training. Final acceptance to the squadron did not come, however, until the recruit had been proven in combat. All members of the C Squadron received static-line parachute training, while almost fifty percent were eventually freefall-trained. The many HALO insertions carried out by the Rhodesian SAS necessitated this large proportion of freefallers. Training in SCUBA and canoe techniques was also included. At least a few members of the Rhodesian SAS additionally received clandestine training with the Israelis in other specialized skills.

In June 1978, C Squadron became the 1st Rhodesian SAS Regiment based at Cranborne near Salisbury. Although now officially a regiment, operational strength of the Rhodesian SAS remained between 150 and 200 men, about the equivalent of two Sabre Squadrons plus support. Even while the Lancaster House talks, which would eventually result in black majority rule, were going on in 1979, the Rhodesian SAS struck into Zambia on a Land Rover raid to kill Joshua Nkomo. Although the raid failed, the strike force did wreck ZIPRA headquarters. The SAS also attempted to kill Robert Mugabe in 1979.

Most SAS members either returned to Great Britain or the United States or crossed the border to South Africa, as the "former" terrorists who now ran Rhodesia had little love for the SAS. Thirty-nine died during the counterinsurgency war and were commemorated on the unit memorial, a memorial spirited out of Zimbabwe to South Africa. Some veterans of the Rhodesian SAS joined or returned to 22nd SAS, bringing their experience of the counterinsurgency war in Rhodesia. A substantial number joined South Africa's Recce Commandos, where a number were killed under odd circumstances on a later raid into Zimbabwe against that country's British-supplied Air Force. Reports within the intelligence community persist that it was a detachment from 22nd SAS sent by the

Members of the Selous Scouts training with Sov Bloc weapons. David Scott-Donelin

British to protect the aircraft that eliminated the raiders. This is speculative, however. What is certain is that within 22nd SAS today, there is no C Squadron; by SAS tradition, that designation belongs to the Rhodesians. When 22nd SAS parades, in fact, they still leave a blank file for C Squadron.

Often confused with the Rhodesian SAS and certainly a unit in the SAS tradition was the Selous Scouts. The Selous Scouts evolved from various units, including the SAS, the Tracker Combat Unit of the Rhodesian Army, the Central Intelligence Organization, and Special Branch of the British South Africa Police. When former SAS member, Major Ron Reid-Daly was given the mission of forming the Selous Scouts late in 1973, infiltration by Communist guerrillas had become endemic. Although the Scouts did do a certain amount of tracking—and this remained their cover mission throughout their existence—their primary mission was to act as a pseudo-terrorist group. Composed of black volunteers from the Rhode-

sian African Rifles-turned terrorists and white volunteers in black face, the Selous Scouts were to infiltrate terrorist operational areas, passing themselves off as a terrorist band. In the process, they would wreak maximum havoc within the terrorist infrastructure.

Drawing on the experience of US Special Forces veterans of the "Road Runner" program in Vietnam and on the experiences with pseudo-gangs in Kenya, the Selous Scouts patterned themselves after the terrorist groups operating in Rhodesia, learning current terminology, identification procedures, and tactics from a constant flow of turned terrorists. As the unit evolved, it undertook other missions, including cross-border raids, assassinations, snatches, and raids on terrorist headquarters outside of Rhodesia. An early and typical Selous Scouts mission was the snatch of an important ZIPRA official from Botswana in March 1974.

The Scouts became experts at ambush, luring terrorists into their traps and either killing them or capturing them. Those captured might

120

be turned and enlisted or they might be turned over to the British South Africa Police for interrogation. As the terrorists in Rhodesia relied heavily on letters for communication, the Scouts often captured a bonanza of intelligence information on the persons of their prey as well. Even better, many of the terrorists were encouraged to keep diaries in their Marxist training camps, once again providing an excellent intelligence source.

Perhaps the closest link between the Selous Scouts and the SAS was the reasoned audacity with which the Scouts carried out their operations. For example, white Selous Scouts would sometimes pose as "prisoners" being transported by black Selous Scouts "terrorists." After being escorted into terrorist strongholds with their "prizes," the Selous Scouts would turn their weapons on the enemy with deadly effect. The most famous and most audacious Selous Scouts raid was on a large ZANLA terrorist camp at Nyadzonya Pungwe in August 1976. Using Unimogs and Ferret Scout Cars painted in FRELIMO camouflage, the eighty-four Selous Scouts drove directly into a large terrorist camp as thousands of terrorists were assembling for morning formation. Using 20mm cannons, .50 MGs, 12.7mm MGs, 7.62mm MGs, and rifles, the Scouts killed an estimated 1,000 terrorists, all for five slightly wounded Selous Scouts. As the strike force retreated back toward Rhodesia, they blew the Pungwe Bridge behind them to frustrate pursuit.

Much of the missions of the Scouts was psychological as they demonstrated to the terrorists that they weren't safe anywhere. Known as the "Skuz'apo" to the terrorists, the Selous Scouts were so feared that it was quite common for two groups of terrorists to begin shooting at each other out of fear that the other group was the Selous Scouts. Such distrust made it more difficult for diverse terrorist groups to carry out joint operations.

Many of the precepts illustrated by Selous Scout successes would be equally valid in analyzing any of the SAS units. First, the Selous Scouts especially illustrated the validity of the statement that calculated audacity will often allow a small counterinsurgency or raiding force to inflict casualties far out of proportion to the unit's numbers. In simple terms, "Who Dares Wins!" Selous Scouts operations also graphically illustrated that terrorists who rely very heavily on fear to gain advantage can themselves be rendered impotent through fear of an enemy who appears suddenly and unexpectedly, hits hard, and then vanishes—who, in effect, turns their own tactics against them.

Selous Scouts' selection also reflected the unit's similarities to the SAS. Perhaps more stress was paid in Selous Scouts' selection to food than in normal SAS selection, however, as during initial selection, the candidate was given one ration pack, but not told what to do with it. As the selection course progressed, this was the only food provided. Those Scouts with initiative foraged around the training area for food, but all grew hungrier by the day. After a few days, an instructor shot a monkey and hung it in the middle of the camp, letting it ripen during subsequent days of training. Finally, as the days of rigorous training and short rations took their toll, the ravenous trainees were treated to the sight of the now maggot-infested monkey being cooked as their first meal in days. Most managed to get it down, in the process learning that if one is hungry enough, protein can be provided from tainted meat, or even maggots. Another useful lesson was that even tainted meat was edible if boiled thoroughly, but it could not be re-heated again. The Selous Scouts were operating in "Indian country," where they could never be sure where their next meal would come from; hence, they trained for this contingency. Land navigation and endurance marches, standard SAS fare, played a key role in Scout selection as well. Weapons training for the Selous Scouts put special emphasis on Communist Bloc weapons as those would be the armament for the pseudo-terrorist groups.

Guile was, however, the most effective weapon in the Selous Scouts arsenal. Their infiltration of enemy camps with "white prisoners" has already been mentioned. Other such operations included the snatching of high-ranking ZIPRA officers in Botswana by posing as

Bots-wana Defense Force soldiers there to arrest them or the launching of fake attacks on farms to establish their terrorist credentials. Some Scouts carried out fake executions of Special Branch informers, establishing reputations as especially ferocious and fearsome terrorists. One of the author's favorite Selous Scouts' cons involved a friend who convinced a terrorist leader he knew had tumbled to his identity that a voice command-detonated explosive device was a radio. The terrorist was told to enter a cave full of terrorists and radio when it was safe for the Scouts to come in. The terrorist, of course, entered the cave, told his cohorts to set an ambush, and then switched on the "radio" and began to call them in. The interior of the cave contained a very complicated terrorist jigsaw puzzle shortly thereafter.

Even after Rhodesia had become Zimbabwe, the Selous Scouts continued to operate from a secret base, smuggling equipment, men, and families to South Africa, where the unit was taken into the South African Defense Forces as no. 5 Recce Commando. The unit then continued to carry out cross-border and pseudo-operations into Mozambique, some members playing a key role in training the Mozambique resistance.

Reconnaissance became an important secondary mission for the Selous Scouts during the later stages of the counterinsurgency campaign. As a result, Chris Shollenberg, a former Rhodesian SAS officer, formed a reconnaissance troop. Operating in small patrols, the troop would set up hides near terrorist camps and gather intelligence. The reconnaissance parties would then either guide in air strikes or Selous Scouts raiding parties.

Unlike most Rhodesian units, the Selous Scouts was fully integrated and egalitarian in the fashion David Stirling foresaw for the SAS. In some cases, blacks commanded whites. Part of Selous Scouts' training was learning the regimental songs—many of which were traditional African, even terrorist songs, which were sung *a cappella*. Not only did this practice give the white Scouts a better understanding of their enemy but also of their black comrades. So effec-

tive was the Scouts system of building *esprit de corps* and loyalty that only once in the entire history of the Selous Scouts did a turned terrorist revert and betray his comrades. The loyalty continued after the cessation of hostilities as well. Realizing that black former Selous Scouts would be in great danger in Zimbabwe, the white Scouts made sure that their black comrades were welcome in no. 5 Recce Commando as well and took them along.

During the counterinsurgency war in Rhodesia, the Selous Scouts either directly or indirectly accounted for sixty-eight percent of all the terrorists killed.

New Zealand SAS

In 1955, a New Zealand SAS squadron (NZ SAS was authorized for service in Malaya to replace C Squadron when it rotated back to Rhodesia. For the new squadron, there were 800 applicants, of which 138 were selected. Under Major Frank Rennie, those selected underwent initial training at Waiourvon on New Zealand's North Island. By December, the squadron had arrived in Malaya, where it underwent parachute training. As with the other SAS units serving in Malaya, the NZ SAS was assigned to track down those Communist Terrorists (CTs) remaining at large. Simultaneously, the squadron was assigned to help move aborigines being terrorized by the guerrillas into protected villages. In the process, the NZ SAS proved quite adept at using turned terrorists as guides and intelligence sources. During an early operation, the NZ SAS killed one of the most sought-after CT leaders, although they lost a trooper in the process.

It was soon found that the New Zealanders did especially well with the aborigines, at least partially due to the presence of the Maori members of the squadron. The NZ SAS also proved especially adept at ambushes. After twenty-four months in Malaya, eighteen of them in the jungle, the squadron began returning to New Zealand in December 1957.

As the squadron had been formed specifically for service in Malaya, it was disbanded upon its return to New Zealand. However, as New

Zealand saw the need for some special operations capability, it was reformed in October 1959. Initially, based on a selection course and some Malayan veterans, one troop was formed at Papakura Army Camp near Aukland. Once selected, the troop underwent weapons, land navigation, and communications training, as well as forced marches with full equipment. Upon completion of this phase, those not already parachute-qualified took jump training with the Australians. A second troop was soon formed, thus bringing the NZ SAS back to squadron status.

On May 17, 1962, the unit was alerted for its first operational deployment to Thailand to fulfill its SEATO obligations as unrest along the Laotian border was perceived as a threat. On May 25, the squadron began loading equipment onto aircraft, leaving the next morning for Australia. After a few days training with the Australians, thirty members of the NZ SAS left for Thailand. The unit was based at Korat with a three-part mission: to show New Zealand support, to learn about Thailand, and to train with the US Special Forces and the Thais. The thirty men were soon broken into two troops, one assigned to work with elements of the US 25th Infantry Division, the other to work with the US Special Forces. Although there turned out to be no combat commitment, the NZ SAS got the chance to hone their skills in jungle operations, reconnaissance, and ambush/counterambush. On September 16, 1962, they returned to New Zealand.

In 1963, the squadron's name was changed to 1st Ranger Squadron, New Zealand SAS in honor of two famous New Zealand military units of the nineteenth century. For the next two years, the squadron carried out intensive training. Then, in February 1965, the NZ SAS was deployed to Borneo in support of the British SAS. Forty members of the squadron were sent to carry out forward reconnaissance, long-range reconnaissance patrols, and hearts-and-minds activities. Members of the NZ SAS were deployed to Sarawak, where they carried out mixed patrols with 22nd SAS and on their own. Other NZ SAS detachments rotated into Borneo

The Rhodesian Selous Scouts' selection course had the reputation of being as tough as that of the SAS and very practical. Here, Rhodesian SAS members undergo parachute training. Rhodesian SAS Association

every few months until September 1966, when the New Zealand commitment wound down as the "confrontation" ended.

Just over two years later, the New Zealanders began their next combat commitment when a twenty-six-man troop was formed to serve with the Australian SAS in Vietnam. After training in Malaysia for jungle warfare and with American weapons, the overstrength troop arrived in Vietnam in December 1968. Their mission was primarily to carry out intelligence gathering and offensive patrols. Like the Australians, the New Zealanders found five-man patrols much more effective than the four-man British SAS patrol or the US Special Forces twelve-man A Detachment. Patrols averaged about ten days, and during their twenty-six months in the country, the NZ SAS carried out 155 patrols. In February 1971, the NZ SAS was withdrawn from Vietnam.

This marked the last combat commitment of the NZ SAS, but the unit continues to train as New Zealand's counterinsurgency, special warfare, and counterterrorist unit. Jungle operations remain a high priority in NZ SAS training, as exercises having been carried out during

Member of the Selous Scouts with a Russian light machine gun illustrates the unit's distinctive camouflage and beret. Note the beard, which helped cover as much of the white face as possible. David Scott-Donelin

the last decade in Malaysia, Brunei, Singapore, Australia, and Fiji.

The last few years have also seen a restructuring of the squadron into the New Zealand SAS Group, comprising two operational squadrons and a training wing. Within the squadrons, troops have the responsibility for either counterterrorism or special warfare, particularly raiding and reconnaissance.

Because the NZ SAS has such wide-ranging special operations responsibilities, selection and training has to be particularly effective. Candidates are drawn from throughout the New Zealand Army, either the regulars or the territorials. Those volunteering and meeting basic requirements next go through a preselection course including psychological testing, physical conditioning, and a review of soldiering skills. Candidates still willing to face selection next go through the actual nine-day selection course which includes swimming, land navigation, and endurance marches. Throughout selection, all movement is at the double-time. The selection course ends with a thirty-five-mile navigation and endurance march, which includes escape and evasion as well as possible "interrogation." Fewer than ten percent of those who begin the process successfully complete selection.

As with the other SAS units, once past selection, the new SAS soldier must complete rigorous training in individual and troop skills. Individual skills include communications, field medicine, patrolling, and combat survival. Once these skills are acquired, the next step is to complete a four-week parachute course. Because of the small size of the NZ SAS, great emphasis is placed on versatility among the unit's members. Nevertheless, three troop specialties are gained during further training: small boat/SCUBA, parachuting (HALO), and tracking. Note that tracking is a specialty not normally present with the other SAS regiments. NZ SAS trackers have such a sound reputation, however, that they are in wide demand to act as instructors for 22nd SAS, the Australian SAS, and the US Special Forces.

In addition to the regular SAS, a territorial SAS unit has been part of the New Zealand Army since 1961. Increased training standards for the Territorial Army (TA) unit within the last few years have upgraded the TA SAS's capability, in effect doubling the available manpower.

Weapons and equipment for the NZ SAS are fairly standard for other SAS units. Standard weapons include the SLR, M-16 and AUG rifles; FN Hi-Power; Minimi; and MP5. The ubiquitous Klepper canoe is also used for waterborne operations.

Australian SAS

The Australians have had an excellent reputation for producing Special Operations Troops at least since the Independent Companies of World War II. Australian infantrymen in general have often been considered "elite" troops in fact. Therefore, when the Australian SAS was formed at Swanbourne, Western Australia, in July 1957, it was to be expected that the unit's quality would be very high. The original mission of the original unit—the 1st SAS Company—was long-range reconnaissance, although the mission was soon expanded to include amphibious operations since the Australians do not have a Marine Corps. Three years later, the company was incorporated into the Royal Australian Regiment. By fall 1964, however, the Australian SAS was a full-fledged regiment with no. 1 and no. 2 Sabre Squadrons, 151 Signals Squadron, and a Headquarters and Base Squadron in charge of administration and training.

From September 1964 to February 1965, squadrons trained in New Guinea, Thailand, and Okinawa. Much of this training, especially in the latter two venues, was carried out with the US 1st Special Forces Group, with whom the Australian SAS has always had particularly strong ties, as the 1st SFG (Abn) has the mission of operating in Asia and the Pacific. Fresh from this jungle training, no. 1 and no. 2 Squadrons were deployed to Borneo in February 1965 for counterinsurgency and cross-border operations. No. 1 Squadron primarily operated in Brunei and no. 2 Squadron primarily operated in Sarawak until the "confrontation" ended in August 1966.

Even before the end of the commitment in Borneo, however, some members of the Australian SAS had been deployed to Vietnam as part of the Australian Army Training Team—Vietnam (AATT-V). Members of the SAS had, in fact, been in Vietnam as early as 1962. A third squadron had been formed and deployed to Vietnam in July 1966. From that date until October 1971, one of the three Australian Sabre Squad-rons and the Signal Squadron would be serving in Vietnam. Normally, the Australian SAS squadron carried out reconnaissance and set ambushes in Phuoc Tuy Province in support of the Australian Task Force. As part of the AATT-V, members of the SAS also carried out training for Vietnamese special forces and for members of the Civilian Irregular Defense Group (CIDG) Program founded by the US Special Forces. As part of the CIDG Program, members of the Australian SAS carried out a typical counterinsurgency hearts-and-minds campaign among the Montagnards, their "bush doctors" proving especially effective at winning friends.

Although the Australian SAS followed the lead of the British SAS in many ways, their typical patrol in Vietnam was normally five men rather than four men: a lead scout, patrol commander, patrol second in command, signaler, and medic. Placing the radio operator and medic toward the rear proved most effective should the patrol run into an ambush. For raids or when setting ambushes, the Australian SAS used multiple patrols. When the Australian SAS left Vietnam, it had the highest kill ratio of any unit that had served in that country.

During the post-Vietnam era, the Australian SAS cut back to two Sabre Squadrons but added a Training Squadron, which also included an Operations Research Unit similar to that of 22nd SAS, as well as a Base Squadron. In the past decade, about one squadron has been assigned to counterterrorist operations. Since the Australian SAS fulfills the functions of both ground and amphibious special forces, however, the counterterrorist mission was for many years split between the Tactical Assault Group (TAG), which would handle missions on land, including aircraft hijackings, and the Off-

shore Installations Assault Group (OAG) for operations on oil rigs or ships. In effect, the TAG carried out those operations that 22nd SAS's SP Team would handle, while the OAG carried out those missions the SBS or Commachio Company of the Royal Marines would handle. In recent years, the OAG designation has been eliminated, with TAG covering the various counterterrorist missions.

As with the other SAS regiments, the Australian SAS has an extremely tough selection course conducted over the deserts of Western Australia. The unit also uses psychological testing during the early stages, but final selection still relies on the tried-and-true rigorous land navigation course. In addition to the usual fatigue factors, the Australian course offers poisonous snakes and crocodiles as hazards. Normally, sixteen percent of officers and twenty-five percent of other ranks pass selection. Once the selection course is passed, candidates for the Australian SAS move into a five-week "familiarization" course with heavy emphasis on training in amphibious operations. Once this phase is finished, candidates move on to a four-week long-range reconnaissance patrol course. Only after completing these two phases do candidates go through a three-week static-line parachute course. Candidates are now ready for their continuation training in demolitions, signals, medics, linguistics, and field engineering. The final phase is training in troop skills, as candidates learn swimming/amphibious (Boat), climbing/rappelling (Mountain), pathfinder/ freefall (HALO), or long-range vehicle operations and maintenance (Mobility). During various phases of training after joining their squadron, SAS soldiers learn survival, team operations, and other skills as well. Survival training includes many traditional aboriginal methods particularly suited to the "defense of Australia" mission. Only upon completion of this entire program does the new member of the Australian SAS Regiment receive his beret and wings.

The Australian SAS, along with no. 1 Commando Regiment, which is a Special Operations Unit within the reserve, falls under the director of special operations. A group of aboriginal

Just as with the SAS, the Selous Scouts put great stress on learning to use Com Bloc weapons. David Scott-Donelin

trackers is also trained by the SAS to assist these two Special Operations Units. When assigned to the counterterrorist mission, Australian SAS squad-rons receive intensive training in the regiment's own "Killing House," as well as on airliners, oil rigs, ships, and buildings.

Weapons include the FAL and M-16, although the AUG is now the standard rifle. The regiment has also used the M-60 general-purpose machine gun, but it is being replaced as well by the FN Minimi. For counterterrorist and certain other special operations, the ubiquitous H&K MP5 is used. For amphibious operations, Kleppers and Zodiacs are the primary craft, and specially equipped Land Rovers, trail bikes, and other vehicles are available.

Perhaps the best summation of just how good the Australian SAS is, is the fact that on more than 1,400 patrols in Borneo and Vietnam involving 298 contacts with the enemy, the Australian SAS killed more than 500 of the enemy with only one man killed and another man missing.

Index